If You Want to Read About Miracles

JOURNEYING OUT OF THE ORDINARY

Nina Lucas

Thank You

There are so many people who have contributed to the richness of our lives. Far too many to mention here but with regards to those helping me compile this book – I would like to thank Barrie, Helen Hawksworth and Jonathan Bugden for their valuable input and expertise. This is the first time I have ventured into this world of writing and they have made it such an enjoyable experience. I am grateful.

Contents

Foreword

Occasionally in life you may meet someone who is, quite simply, an extraordinary person. An even greater blessing is when that meeting leads to a precious and profound friendship with them. This is exactly what happened to us when we encountered Nina and her husband Barrie – it was like we had known them forever! The love, care, and compassion they exude is an inspirational example to all who know them and is also echoed and seen in the hearts and lives of their children and grandchildren. This book tells their story, and how loving God and others led them and their family to 'journey beyond the ordinary'. There is a sign in the Lucas kitchen, 'This family runs on love, laughter and lots of cups of tea'. That is what happens on a daily basis and we have witnessed it up close and personal. Enjoy the read – you will find hilarity, profundity, and their joy at being part of the family of an extraordinary God.

Jonathan and Pam Bugden

Introduction

I have felt for some time that I should write a book. I did not want some of the events of our lives to slip away into the mist and be forgotten. Our story is one about ordinary people who found a relationship with an extra ordinary God. Some people may find these events hard to believe and if I had not witnessed them for myself, I too would find it difficult to grasp. The facts are written here for all to see and I hope they will encourage others to believe they can live a life outside of the ordinary.

Please note; – I have changed the names of all the people that I can no longer contact to get their permission to use their real names.

PART 1

I can remember years ago reading that Abraham[1]. left Ur of the Chaldeans in search of the city with foundations, whose architect and builder was God[2]. Archaeologists have excavated the area of Ur and found houses dating back to Abraham's time and they had water, heating and were like a very simple, modest houses of our own time. Abraham and family left all these wonderful amenities, family and community to live in a tent.

He was searching to find the most beautiful, glorious city one could imagine – the perfect city of God.

Well, here I am sitting in our study looking out on the snow falling on the houses and gardens creating a clean, sparkling view of our neighbourhood. In some of these houses however, are people who are suffering in many ways. I can relate to Abraham's desire to follow God and find a city free from pain, sickness and hurt. The most perfect place.

So, the journey begins . . .

1

A Little Bit About Myself

I was born in 1946, at home, to loving parents and older sister in the city of Hull. Apparently, my parents kept a duck in the back yard which contracted pneumonia and died, with some quacking and lots of fuss, the night I was born. The midwife was called and checked mum over but felt it would be some time yet and wanted to leave; but Dad locked the door, hid the door key in his trousers and would not let her out until mum had given birth. From the information passed down it sounded like chaos, but I was delivered safely, and all was well.

I was educated in Hull, and passed, (what was then called) the 11+, and went to an all-girls grammar school, 'Estcourt High'. My parents could not afford to let me stay on in the six form. They needed extra finances so, I needed some sort of paid employment to contribute to the house keeping. Night-school was the only way to continue with my education so I enrolled at the tech and studied A level Maths and Chemistry.

I got a job in a laboratory as a lab assistant and for two years experienced my first real exposure to the world outside of school and home. As part of the job, I had to go into the factory to take samples for spot checks, however the Lab staff were not always well received by some of the factory workers, and we were frequently threatened with a beating after hours. Fortunately, it never happened!

Wanting something more from my labours, I applied to go to the Leeds School of Radiography and started my training in 1965. I think it shocked my Dad that I was going to leave home, because he could not look after me at a distance. He believed that it was a waste of time and money to educate women past a certain point as they would get married and have children and that would be the end of any career. In the hope of dissuading me he told me that 'If you go, you are on your own and you will not get any help from me'. He was true to his word. When asked by the interviewers at the Leeds school of Radiography if my parents were happy to support me, as I would need extra financial help to supplement the bursary. I lied and said yes. I was so determined. I did a little sewing to help with the costs; I walked everywhere in all weathers to save bus fares. Leeds was a big city and the hospitals we were sent to were spread out. Somehow it did not mater, I was doing what I really wanted to do.

Just to back track a little; As a teenager I had started going to St Columba's church and youth club where I met my husband of over 50 years, Barrie. At first, I did not really like him as I thought he was a goody two shoes, and not really very exciting. On top of this, he had (what I considered to be) the most awful taste in clothes. It seemed an important issue at that time. We started dating nearly a year before I went to Leeds and his support and encouragement helped me a lot. My brother George was a welcome (but late) arrival to the family. He was born prematurely the year before I went to college. Wow did he challenge mum and dad as he did not seem to like sleep and for the most part had only 20-minute catnaps. I don't know how they survived but survive they did. George is not like that now.

Once in Leeds my training began and I stayed for a few months in a YWCA (Young Women's Christian Association). Radiography students had to find their own accommodation, unlike the nurses. However, once I had made friends, four of us rented a flat together and had a great time working, studying, and socialising together. This group comprised of art graduate (doing a post graduate teaching course), two physio students and me, all learning to cook, wash and shop in the market for cheap food.

Whilst learning we made many mistakes. One week there was some milk left over. Not wanting to waste it, I thought I would have a go at making cheese before it went off. After a few weeks of it stinking and smelling the flat out, I gave in and threw it away much to the relief of my flat mates. Was that a failure or just a learning curve?

My flat mate who was doing a post graduate teaching course, was helping at St Georges Crypt as part of her thesis. It was a place for the homeless and she was helping with the 'down and outs' as we called them at that time. The homeless people could stay for three nights, sleep on benches or on cardboard on the floor. At least they were out of the cold and elements. They would be served soup on arrival. Any bottles of alcohol were confiscated on entry and returned on leaving. Medical issues were looked at, their feet washed, and blisters and sores dressed. When she invited me to go with her, I initially refused but later changed my mind as I was curious about what she was doing.

As a helper, I was asked to interview the men to find out why they were there and if we could help in any way. Some of the more seasoned guests would see me coming. They perceived a young person, with little or no experience of life and really tried to take me for a ride with stories that were far from the truth. It was clear that they were hurting so I had to learn quickly but be kind. I saw the selfless devotion of the staff working in difficult, dirty, and smelly conditions. It was here that I began to see many things differently. I began to attend St Georges Church when I could, looking for answers. It was also here that I took classes and was confirmed. I had begun to read my Bible, an old King James version with tiny print, but I read it through twice understanding so little of what I was reading. I felt like the Ethiopian Eunuch written about in the Bible. He was reading from the book of Isaiah but did not understand what he was reading and needed someone to explain it to him[3].

When it seems as if people have been thrown together through circumstances, some say that it is coincidence. But I began to feel that these happenings were not coincidences but 'God Incidences'. It amazed me how my flat mates and I supported one-another, and I really appreciated these lovely young women. (I am so pleased to say that these friends all did well in their chosen paths)

As mentioned, the training involved far more than learning in the School of Radiography and the practical experience in the hospitals to which students were sent. It involved other skills important for being able to survive in the world.

The course was divided into two main parts with an exam at the end of each part. I found it fascinating. There was so much to learn and explore and I was determined to make the most of it. Not everything was plain sailing however, the Nursing Practice Module, which was included in Part 1, was a challenge. The nursing tutor's feedback included the discouraging statement that I was illiterate. I had made some spelling mistakes in a paper I submitted. So rather than feel sorry for myself or angry, I worked harder and guess what? I got a distinction in the exam. The tutor's comments afterwards were that it was either a fluke or that it was a miracle, I'll leave you to guess. The Lord was so good to me even though I had not made any commitment to Him at that point and I won a prize for my work at the end of both Part 1 and

Part 2. I qualified with flying colours and was offered a job at St James Hospital Leeds.

Joy of joys, when I was invited to address the new students, families, and the school of Radiography at our graduation ceremony, my Mum and Dad were there. Here at last I saw that my Dad was proud of me, a daughter.

2

Faint Heart Never Won Fair Lady

Barrie left school at 14 years old and took up a seven-year apprenticeship as a Shipwright and Boat Builder with a ship repairing company in Hull. His training embraced several disciplines, carpentry, joinery, lofts man, and had insights into engineering. He had worked as a voluntary Youth Leader in Hull and found the work fulfilling. As a result, he wanted to train to be a professional youth and community worker. Whilst I was in Leeds, Barrie went to Leister University to do his Youth and Community training. We met as frequently as we could despite the distance and financial restrictions. Many letters were exchanged, some of which I have today.

As our relationship was becoming serious, I was getting increasingly scared. I did not know if I could sustain a relationship. Would he still like me when he knew how grumpy and upside down, I could be? Would I be able to be a good wife and hold down the career I really enjoyed? The career that I had invested so much in. Many, I am sure, will relate to these questions and the struggles in times of indecision. I tried at one point to gently bring the relationship to a close, but Barrie visited me again whilst I was home for a weekend. He was obviously so upset, and I was shocked. I had not realising that someone could love me that much and show such courage without trying to push me into anything. He simply stated his case and gave me time to make up my mind. He did however ask me to give him an answer by the Christmas when I was due to go home for the holiday. Christmas came and Barrie was waiting for me as my train pulled into the station at Hull. His words were, as I stepped off the train, well is your answer yes, or no? No wasting time there then! I found myself saying, 'Yes'.

That night I was overwhelmed. Oh! what had I done? As I settled down for the night in my parents' home, I was praying and unable to sleep. I heard a voice say:

It is Ok, it will all work out. He is the right one.

I had never heard the audible voice of God. I did not even know it was possible in modern times. Peace came over me and the following days together were lovely.

We did not want to get married until we had both completed our courses and passed our exams. So, it was important to pass and not have to wait to take a re-sit. When we qualified, I had manged to save £45. Barrie on the other hand was in debt to the tune of £44. So, we shared the money out and were both debt free, but we did need to earn some money. Even back then, getting married and setting up home was expensive. Fortunately, our needs were modest.

We set the wedding day for June 1st (1968), and by that time I had worked for 5 months as a qualified radiographer at St James hospital. Barrie had been in post for a year as a youth and community worker, at Westfield Folk House in Mansfield Nottingham. Obviously one of us had to move and Barrie had a flat that went with the job. I applied for a post at Mansfield General Hospital which was just across the road from the youth centre. It was so sad to say goodbye to my friends and colleagues in Leeds. It felt a bit like leaving home, but I was really proud to have been part of the work there, even for just a few short years.

So many changes, a new town, newly married, and a new job. It was both a difficult time and an exciting one. Because of Barrie's work, many people in the town already knew him. When we walked down-town to do our shopping, people would greet him by name – but no one knew me at that point. This did not feel much like home.

Trying to be a good wife was also a challenge. It meant one thing to Barrie and another to me. For example, I thought that a good wife cooked her husband breakfast every morning. (not sure where that came from) But one morning I had been up early and cooked breakfast. I served it up in the kitchen and Barrie would not even get out of bed to eat it. He had breakfast in bed that morning, minus the plate. I'll leave that to your imagination. Now if breakfast in bed is mentioned to him now, his expression says it all!

There were many events that took place at the youth centre and the Friday night dance/disco was a regular. The young people came in all their best or trendy gear and queued outside the centre. They were visible from the kitchen window of our first-floor flat, which overlooked the foyer entrance.

The foyer was mostly glass with a flat roof. If I had any left-over bread or cake, I would break it up into bits and throw it onto the flat roof for the birds to eat. This particular evening there was the usual noise and excitement of large numbers of young people gathering outside the Centre. I was just clearing away after our evening meal and had some fresh cream cakes that would not last another day. As usual I thought I'll throw them out for the birds. I opened the kitchen window and just as I threw the cakes and crumbs out, a gust of wind took them in the wrong direction. The bits were blown down onto the young people underneath, cake and cream. Oh, they were so surprised. They all looked up. I did not know what to do, so I ducked underneath the window sill and hid until the uproar died down.

Wanting to try new things, I thought that I would try making bread. I had never done it before, so with recipe and instructions in hand, I had a go. Hours later it still had not risen. It was getting close to bedtime, so I put it in the oven anyway. It was solid and far too hard to eat even for the determined. Well, there was always the foyer roof and the hungry birds. However, the birds were not able to make a dent in it. Even after weeks, months, perhaps even a year, there was still no sign of interest from our feathered friends. Even the weather had failed to soften its crust. Don't know how this happened but fortunately later attempts proved more successful.

Working at Mansfield General, although it was conveniently just across the road, had other challenges. Here also I was the new girl on the block. I had arrived with glowing references which can be a disadvantage, as there is more to live up to. Perhaps some of the people who would have been friendly, find you more of a challenge.

I had been used to a level of respect in the way staff treated each other and others, but here it was a very different situation. It was not a happy place for me and after 18 months I applied for a senior post at Nottingham City Hospital. A radiographer had to be qualified for three years before becoming eligible for a senior role and I had been qualified for only two. During the interview the Superintendent of the department said:

If I gave you the job, you will be managing people who have been qualified longer than yourself. Those who feel that they should have been given the post. How will you cope with that situation?

I replied that it could not be any worse than what I had experienced in the last 18 months. He must have been satisfied with my answer and gave me the job. It had to be as 'an acting up' senior until I had been qualified three years after which he authenticated the senior role. There were difficulties, as he had indicated, but I loved it there. The level of care that was shown to patients and staff was genuine, progressive, and excellent. The superintendent and deputy were amazing and such a good team. The superintendent did everything at a rate of knots, even eat. I did wonder if he slept by speeding up two hours into one! I was at home there and it was here that I began to learn about ultrasound and nuclear medicine and did courses on both. What a privilege to be part of what was then, new and ground-breaking work.

3

New Home

When we had been married three years, we began to feel that it was time to think about starting a family. Our first floor flat, in the old building on the side of the youth centre did not seem like the ideal place to rear children. We were sharing the bathroom and toilet with the two bed sits on the third floor and really felt that we wanted a house with a bit more privacy and a garden. Neither of us had any idea what sort of house we could get for our money. We did not even know what we could borrow as a mortgage or how it all worked. There was a lot to learn but we found out how much we could borrow and then visited an estate agent who gave us several brochures of places to go and see. We had asked for older properties, thinking we could get more space for our money. If work was required, we would do it ourselves as we were quite good at DIY. However, nothing we looked at seemed right. He had suggested that we go and look at a new property in a village called Wellow but we declined for the above reason, it was new. We did however have some very funny experiences looking at places and trying to compare them to the written descriptions we were given.

Oak Dene, for example, was described as a house of character with stained glass window in the front door. That bit at least was correct. It pointed out features like a cocktail bar in the corner of the front room, a lean-to green house with grape vine, fully tiled bathroom (with large useful airing cupboard on the landing) and a fully fitted kitchen. Now let me tell you what we found – There were steps leading up to the front door which had a window panel of stained-glass. It looked more like the side entrance to some old church building and I commented that it did not seem very homely. Next, the hallway and stairs revealed so much damp that the wallpaper was billowing away from the wall. It had been secured in places by staples. I say 'had been' because as we walked in some of the staples gave way and a huge strip of paper was released, floating down from top to bottom! Now into the front room. The cocktail bar was a plank of 'nine by one' wood nailed across the corner of the room! By this time, we got the giggles and as we mounted the stairs to have a look, the intensifying smell of damp met us. It was everywhere in the empty bedrooms. The bathroom, what could be wrong with that? We opened the door to watch the last remaining tiles fall from the ceiling into the bath! What started out as a giggle was becoming full blown laughter. The airing cupboard was amazing, it was made by nailing 'Landers Bread Trays' together and we could still read 'Landers Bread' stamped into the wood. Well just to complete the experience we ventured outside through the kitchen, nearly tripping over the uneven tiles on the kitchen floor. The lean-to green house was being held up by the out of control, rampant grape vine and had very little glass left in it to give any shelter to frost sensitive plants. You can guess that we did not go for that house but on the way out, the stained-glass window in the door did not look so bad.

Back to the estate agent and he again said:

I think you should go and have a look at the new property in Wellow. It is between two villages with older properties you could look at, so it will not be out of your way.

He thrust the details into Barrie's hand and off we went. To cut a long story short we drove past the new property, which was an empty, four-bedroom Dorma bungalow with a third of an acre of land. The builders had not finished everything, even though it had been occupied for a few months. The outside woodwork was still covered with primer. The garden which had been a field had not been touched, it was still in its original state. We loved it! Now knowing the price of properties, we thought that this would be well outside of our price range.

Do you believe in miracles? Well one was about to happen. The owner of this bungalow, a mining engineer, had emigrated to South Africa. Although several people had wanted to buy this property, they had been unable to contact the owner to secure a deal and as a result backed out. He had left instructions that it should not be sold for less than £4,600 but was on the market for £6,000. Don't laugh, it sounds ridiculous now. The maximum that we could borrow was £3,700. Now here's the miracle. It just so happened that the Secretary of the youth centre where Barrie worked, had a solicitor friend who had emigrated to the area that this mining engineer was working. The secretary contacted his solicitor friend, who in turn contacted the owner. Now the many delays had worked in our favour. The owner really was ready to sell, and he was willing to part with the property for £3,700. We had our new home and could not stop smiling.

That night in 1971, the night that we moved in Barrie could not sleep. The responsibility of owing that amount of money and having to pay it back, weighed very heavily on him. He tossed and turned in bed disturbed by every unfamiliar noise. I on the other hand was excited but slept like a log.

We started to think about a name for our new home and many ideas came to mind but the one that stuck was 'Columba Folk'. If you remember we met at St Columba's Church youth club. We married at St Columba's Church, so it seemed like a good name although we did not realise the significance of it at the time. Some of you may know the story of this amazing Irish monk, St Columba. He with his companions sailed from Ireland in small boats that were barely seaworthy across an extremely rough stretch of sea. Leaving home behind they landed on the Scottish island of Iona in 563AD. From there they established a monastic base, teaching, healing etc and even evangelised parts of Scotland. More on this later.

Well, we now had a huge garden and neither of us knew anything about gardening. A retired police inspector who lived down the road with his lovely wife, took us under their wing. He gave us lots of hints and tips and bedding plants! He was also a game keeper looking after some nearby woods. Sometimes we would find a brace of pheasants on the doorstep or a rabbit or two. Feeling very inadequate I had to confess that as a towny, I had no idea what to do to prepare these animals for the pot. Even that did not deter him, he asked his wife to do it for us and nicely prepared joints arrived with a little note on how to cook them! I think he liked us.

The small but very pretty village had a shop, a private school, a riding school, a post office, two pubs and last but not least two churches. One being an Anglican church St Swithin's and the other a Methodist Chapel, but its real claim to fame was a May Pole which sat proudly on the village green. The village's May day celebrations drew people from all over the area.

We made many friends in Wellow. It was a happy place to live and learn. We started to attend St Swithin's and I even got to sing in the choir with hat, robes and all!

Our first child, Helen, was born in the summer of 1973 a couple of months after leaving work. (Over the next seven years she was joined by Kate, then Erica and Esther. This completed our family of six). Helen was beautiful with blue eyes and dark hair the colour of a raven's wing. I used to just look at her and wonder, is she really ours? Now in her forties she is still beautiful and her hair just as dark. A week after she was born Barrie had to go to Germany for two weeks as part of his job. He was taking a youth group on an exchange. Every other year Mansfield would send a group to Heiligenhaus in the Ruhr and the following year would receive a youth group from Germany. Mansfield had twinned with this town and the youth exchange was only one event amongst many that were organised to sponsor good relationships between the two towns and countries. I found it hard not having Barrie around. We both felt that the demands on a youth and community worker at that time were not compatible to family life. The next process of change began. Barrie applied for teacher training and started his course at Retford an outpost for Nottingham University in 1975.

4

A Very Special Neighbour

Our house was last but one going out of the village towards Ompton and Newark. We were on a hill and close to a bend in the road. Infront and behind us were farmers' fields. Living in the last property, which was a bungalow with an acre of land, were a young couple with two children. Not long after the youngest was born in early 1975, the husband Jon, had an accident on a building site and broke his ankle. Not a serious thing you might be tempted to think, but he developed a thrombosis and died leaving our neighbour Tina on her own with these two lovely little girls. One was aged three and the other six months. We were very moved by this, shocked at just how suddenly someone could be taken away. I really wanted to be a friend, get a bit closer, but was not sure how. I felt awkward and was worried I would say something thoughtless and inadvertently upset them. After Jon's death, the local Methodist minister would call for about 10 minutes every day to see them, and check if there was anything she needed.

A couple of months later we noticed that there were several cars parked outside her house every Monday evening. We thought perhaps it was a Sunday School meeting as we knew Tina was involved in the Methodist church. One Tuesday evening I saw her on the drive and mentioned that If her Sunday school visitors needed a place to park, they could use our drive. Thank you, she replied and told me that it was not a Sunday school meeting, it was a fellowship meeting. I asked her what that was?

Tina said 'It is a meeting for worship, prayer and sharing' and she added, 'You can come if you would like to'.

I wanted to get to know her better so I said that I would and asked her what time it started? The answer was 7pm. I shared this conversation with Barrie, and he thought that it did not sound very stimulating and that one hour on a Sunday morning was enough for him.

The following Monday evening, I went next door and the unexpected happened. The group was very interdenominational, Pentecostals, Anglicans, and Methodists, both male and female. They sang unaccompanied, which I admit, was a bit hit and miss, but when they prayed, they spoke to God as if He was really there. To add to that, they thanked Him for answering the prayers they had prayed last week. This was also a new concept; God actually answering prayers. One man was speaking words I did not recognise, and I thought he was foreign, but then he spoke with a normal accent, so what was this? I was fascinated, and really excited by it all with many questions and far from being bored or uninspired.

In the meantime, Barrie was getting a bit worried. He had expected the meeting to last not more than an hour. You know like the Sunday service in and out in an hour, but after 8pm, 9pm 10pm had passed, he was still waiting. What could be going on, what are they doing all this time? At ten fifteen pm I walked into the kitchen and was on such a high with it all, he could not take it in. He reached the conclusion that they must be a group of nutters to have this effect on his wife and that he would check it out the following week.

Next Monday arrived and off Barrie went. He had been very sceptical but could see instantly, that these people had a real relationship with the God that he could only acknowledged might exist, somewhere out there. As a result, we both wanted to go on Monday evenings and needed to find a babysitter. We did not have much money as Barrie was on a student's grant, so we needed someone who would do it for love! This was the start of another journey. We were both really hungry for a relationship with the very present, very real God.

One day as Barrie was cutting the grass in the front garden, the Methodist minister passed by on his way to visit Tina. Barrie could see that he wanted to talk, so stopped what he was doing and went over to him. Tom asked:

If I invited you both for supper, would you come?

Barrie said of course we would. So, they set a date for the following Friday evening. Now to Yorkshire folk like us, supper means a sandwich or perhaps a piece of cake before you go to bed, so we had fish and chips for our evening meal before we set off. On arrival we noticed that the table was set for several courses. Not a sandwich then? Panic set in, how are we going to eat all this and not upset them as they had gone to so much trouble. Tom and his wife were very gracious and when the meal was over and cleared away, we sat by a roaring open fire to chat.

Tom asked: Are you Christians?

Barrie replied: Yes, I think so.

Tom said that it was the wrong answer. We thought, what does he mean? Tom continued:

Do you know the Lord Jesus as your Saviour?

Barrie: Yes, I think so.

Tom said: No, that is the wrong answer, you either know or don't know, not just think so. Let me put it another way. If it was possible to know the Lord Jesus personally, would you want to?

Barrie replied: If you put it like that yes, I would.

Tom said: Why don't you then?

Barrie: I don't know how. I echoed the same response.

Tom; If I lead you in a prayer to accept Jesus as your Lord and Saviour, would that help?

Well, the rest is history, we could not wait to get to know Jesus. Tom explained that we needed to renounce any involvement in the occult. Then ask for forgiveness for any know sin in our lives and forgive anyone who had hurt us in any way. This done, we prayed. We both felt so incredibly hot, almost unbearably hot. We thought it was the result of the second meal or the open fire but the Holy Spirit had touched us, cleansed us and filled us. Things were never going to be the same again. I have included a similar prayer at the end of the book if you also want to know the Lord Jesus for yourself[4].

On the way home we were both euphoric. It was a clear night, and the moon was bright. We could see rabbits in the hedge row, and everything looked like a Walt Disney cartoon. What had just happened? The next morning Barrie got up to make a cup of tea and routinely look up the daily bible reading notes that many Anglicans read. What had previously seemed a bit bland, flat like a small black and white television screen, burst into Cinema screen – glorious technicolour. He was blown away. I just wanted to pray and sing all the time. A change had taken place in us both and I found that I had feelings of love towards people who previously had hurt or annoyed me. We had been 'Born Again'.

Tina was so delighted when we told her and mentioned that perhaps if she had prayed harder, it could have happened sooner. This dear lady had been through the grief of losing her husband, caring for two little ones on her own and had been praying for Barrie and I. I thought, this is sacrificial love. She was willing in this way, to lay down her life for us, to put aside her own feelings and care about our lives and salvation. Over a cup of tea one afternoon Tina said:

Do you know who I want to see first when I get to heaven?

I was thinking she was going to say Jon as they really loved each other and were very close. But she went on to say:

It is Jesus, yes, I know what you were thinking. I do want to see Jon, but I want to see Jesus first. Jesus is the one who laid down His life and made the sacrifice for us. He is the One caring for Jon now.

This impacted me. I started to think about How I would feel. Would Jesus be my first choice?

Tina experienced the baptised in Holy Spirit[5]. In simple words, this means the presence of Gods Holy Spirit came on and around her, like she was immersed in Him, like water at a baptism. She was mowing her lawns at the time, an acre of them and singing hymns and choruses. She found herself singing in a language she had not learned. I don't think she had asked God for this blessing, but she had honoured Jesus with the first place in her life, so her focus was on Him, i.e., the giver, not the gifts He brings. I know that Holy Spirit brings glory and honour to Jesus and this was Tina's heart also, so I thought that Holy Spirit would feel at home with Tina.

About year after Jon had died, it was on a Saturday morning that Tina seemed to be having trouble getting her car started. *Barrie* is going to take the story from here: –

Tina's drive was on a slope. I remember that Tina used to release the hand brake and free wheel down the drive and sharp turn to position the car level with the road. She would then start the engine to drive off. This particular morning the car would not start. The starter motor was running but there was no life in the engine. I went out to see if I could help. I asked her if the car had been serviced recently and she informed me that the last time was when Jon had had it serviced. That had to be about 18 months ago. I asked her if she would like me to service it for her and she said:

Oh, that would be kind of you.

She had intended to go shopping, so she gave her brother a ring to come and pick her up along with the girls and take them to the shops.

Having sorted out some tools to tackle this rather dead Singer Gazelle, I lifted the bonnet. I could see immediately why the engine would not start; there was no electrical connection to the ignition coil. The cable had not just come lose; it was non-existent. It must have fallen off some time ago as the connector that should have been clean and shiny, was now well oxidised. It had obviously been missing for quite some time. On the way up the drive to the garage I popped my head round the kitchen door and said to Nina:

I've found the problem and no wonder it would not start, it couldn't!

I tried to explain it to her but well, that's not her gift but she knew that I was excited about something. I had all the parts to make up a new cable and having done that, I decided to check the spark plugs. I removed the first one expecting to find that the gap would need to be adjusted, but there was no gap to adjust, the anode was completely burnt away. The other three spark plugs were just the same! For any of these plugs to make a spark they would have required more energy than any car would be capable of producing. I now needed four new sparkplugs. I though I better just check the distributor. When I removed the cap, I touched the distributor arm. I was surprised to find it was rotating freely instead of being locked on to the rotor; the keyway had broken off and was nowhere to be seen. I stood there totally bewildered as this car could not have started, not just because of one fault but three!

Some months earlier friends that lived down our road, had emigrated to Canada. Doug had left me a box of bits from his garage which I had put in my garage unopened. I did not have the compatible spares to repair Tina's car but thought to look in

Doug's box. I found four brand new spark plugs still in their boxes, that would fit a Singer Gazelle. I began to feel that I was witnessing miracle after miracle. It was uncanny, more than just coincidence. However, neither box had a replacement rotor arm, and it was now Saturday afternoon. All the car spare shops were closed now until Monday. I had noticed that a garage and petrol station in Ollerton (the next village) had several car spares on display near the till. I called in to see if by some remote chance they had a rotor arm for a Singer Gazelle. They had everything but not that specific one. I was just on my way out when the man behind the counter asked:

Did you find what you were looking for?
No: I replied.
Hang on a minute, just have a look in here.

He pulled out a big draw at the back of the counter filled with hundreds of bits and pieces and sure enough right on the top, a rotor arm for a Singer Gazelle. I did not even have to rummage for it. He gave it to me and would not take anything for it. When I got back, I fitted the rotor arm, the spark plugs, cable, checked the water and the oil, put the key in the ignition and the engine sprang into life.

When Tina returned home, she was so pleased that I had repaired and serviced the car for her and that it was now working. I asked her if she had had problems starting it before. She looked rather sheepish and said that she had. I asked her: How did you manage to start it?

She coloured up and said that she would put her hands on the bonnet and ask God to start it for her. I knew that was the only way it could have started!

I was so pleased that God demonstrated His love for Tina by working miracles to start her car but at the same time realised that God was speaking to me. He used the things I understood and showed me miracles I could comprehend. It was like He was speaking in my language to reveal His love for me.

Tina's brother Jim was also a blessing. One Monday evening, at the end of our fellowship meeting, Jim told us that he had been praying that day. The Lord had given him a Scripture that he thought was for us. He told us what it was but as it was late, we decided to look at it the following day. On Tuesday evening, having put the Helen and Kate to bed, we opened our Bibles to look up the reference. Now what did Jim say? We found the verse that we thought he had mentioned and read about 'Speaking the truth in love'[9]. This initiated a conversation that neither of us expected.

Somehow, it was like the flood gates opened and I unleashed all the petty things that Barrie had done or was doing that annoyed me. There seemed to be more than I had realised, and they came out one after the other in quick succession. It was like cashing in a book of Green Shield Stamps. Some may remember that years ago, these stamps were given in shops, petrol stations etc in proportion to how much you had spent. Each stamp was basically worthless on its own but a book full was worth something.

Then another surprise, Barrie shared all his niggles. I had never realised Barrie had these feelings. He had never shared them. After the initial shock of all this, we decided that from that moment, we would keep a short account of our annoyances. Where possible we would not let the sun go down on our anger. Each week we set aside time to share meaningfully with each other, the things that gave us the 'Oooch' feeling and other things we needed to address. This has worked well for us. It has brought us closer together and given us understanding that we would not otherwise have developed. I did not share in love, more in anger. I did it all wrong and would not recommend that way to others. But this is how it happened. Although it was painful for a while, God worked it out for our good.

The following Monday evening we told Jim what had happened after reading the Scripture he had given us and he was surprised also. The Scripture we read was not the one he had passed on! That was strange! Well God has His own plans.

Another Strange but Chilling Occurrence.

We could pray in every room in our home except one, the dining room. It was odd but there was a colder atmosphere in this room. To add to this, twice we had other unexplainable occurrences. My electric sewing machine was sitting on a table in the corner of this room and twice it started to run without anyone being near it. I thought at first it was a surge in the mains electricity but on inspection, the plug was complete with a fuse and everything was in order. So, what was happening?

We wondered if there was something we had brought in that was linked with the occult. We had a brass topped table with some sort of oriental writing around the edge. It looked so attractive, but we were not sure what the writing said so we got rid of that. We had some black ebony salad servers with strange heads carved on the ends and we were not sure about them either, so they went. We had a Buddhist wheel of life that came from Nepal and we had no need of that, so it got thrown out. I bet the men that collected our rubbish thought it was there lucky day. But there was still no change of atmosphere in the room.

On the wall above my sewing table there was a large brass plaque that was a gift from relatives. It had a drinking scene in the centre, with two men in old fashioned costume sitting at a table holding large beer tankards in their hands. It had a deep border of closely entwined flowers and fruit around its edge. Barrie was looking at it and he just so happened to notice that at the bottom of this elaborate flower and fruit border was Satan's head. It was so well concealed in amongst the design that neither of us had seen it. Once that was removed and destroyed, the room was peaceful again. We could pray in there and we never had another weird occurrence.

5

Repercussions

To our surprise, the reactions to our good news of getting to know Jesus, were very mixed. My Dad just said:

Whatever makes you happy but leave me out of it.

Barrie's Dad however refused to talk to us for a couple of years and his mum said nothing. Barrie's brother was angry. We were not sure why. He was certainly fearful that we had joined some sort of cult because after all, to go to church on a Sunday is one thing but for it to change your life is another. My sister and brother-in-Law initially seemed indifferent, but later there were some interesting developments. Things were very challenging at times.

We endeavoured to share our experience with the then vicar of St Swithin's but he did not seem to know what we were talking about and it became obvious that he had not experienced being born again. He served the community as best he could but from that moment on, he made it perfectly obvious that he did not approve of us or what we wanted to do or share. Jesus gave us love and patience and eventually some things changed.

Let me start with my sister and brother-in-law. They lived in the next but one village to us. They had moved with their three children from Hull because of the shortage of jobs in that area. Alan got a job as a trainee blacksmith at a local colliery. It was lovely to have them so close. We asked them if they would like to come to dinner with us and the local Methodist minister Tom and his wife and surprise, surprise, they all came. Just before they all went home, Tom asked Alan if he was a Christian? The conversation that followed mirrored in some ways the conversation Tom had had with Barrie and I, when he led us to accept Jesus as our Saviour. Alan prayed the prayer and gave his life to the Lord. On the way-out he said:

I don't know if I have done the right thing.

Too late: we replied.

It was not long before both he and my sister, were both well and truly in love with Jesus.

Alan became a local Methodist preacher and worked with SASRA (Soldiers and Airmen's Scripture Readers Association) following his years in the TA Paratroopers division. They have both been involved ever since, serving the Lord and His people in local churches. What a joy to be able to talk about the things of God with family. Alan has an anointing for evangelism, and one after the other people came to know the Lord. There was so little in the area to encourage these people, so we formed a group for adults which met in Alan and Heather's home. We were soon packed out, over thirty people all worshiping, together. Barrie would sometimes bring a word. Simon, a concert pianist would play, and you could tell when he moved from playing to worship. It was like God flicked a switch. Alan played his guitar and sang. It was a welcome oasis in the area.

The next event in the family was as follows.

My mother was really upset when my Grandma's brother, my great uncle Sid died. He was the last of that generation. Mum had looked after him and they were close. The night of his death my mum physically felt God rock her to sleep. What had been just head knowledge regarding things of God became a reality, and her walk with Jesus really took off.

Who's next you might ask? Well, my younger brother came with us on holiday to Trusthorpe. We were camping with a group from the fellowship next door plus Heather (my sister) and Alan. Tina's brother led my little brother to the Lord. He was aged 13 at the time. We were still praying for my dad but nothing seemed to be happening but let me tell you a little of his story.

Both dad and mum had been in the navy during the 2nd World war. They were both petty officers. Dad was on minesweepers; a very dangerous job and mum did the books for the admiral. Whilst dad was out at sea, he became very ill and was taken to a field hospital in Singapore. The doctors there realised that, if they did not operate and remove a very damaged kidney, he would die. With limited resources and probably limited skills, they removed his kidney and sent him home not expecting him to live. He did recover but was told that he must work outside in the fresh air and get built up as he was so thin and had little appetite. The scar stretched from his spine at the back around his abdomen to the middle of the front. Even as a radiographer I had never seen a scar that long, it looked like he had been cut in half. We had to be careful not to hug or touch him there, for even after many years he was understandably still very sensitive in that area. From that time on he had problems with his back. Muscles that supported his vertebrae had been severed leaving a weakness. This resulted in him spending increasing amounts of time flat on his back in bed, with boards under the mattress. Well, from one January to the following Easter he had been laid up. The doctor said that he would never work again, and he had a corset fitted which stretched from under his arms to just below his hips. For dad, not to be able to work was a big blow. He was so independent. But with this corset he could manage to drive. Mum was missing the family so much that he drove from Hull to Nottinghamshire. This two-hour drive was no small achievement and they arrived safely at lunch time on the Friday.

The timing of this visit presented us with a dilemma. We were so pleased to see them after what seemed like a long time, but we felt a bit torn as we wanted to go to a Christian healing meeting that evening. So, how do we tell dad? The meeting was at a place called Kellam Hall just a few miles away. It used to be a monastery but was now owned by the council who hired it out for functions. We said to dad that we realised that it must have been a really challenging day for him. We quite understood if he felt he needed to rest. If he wanted to stay home one of us would gladly stay and keep him company but several of us would like to go to a healing meeting.

Well, the first miracle of the day happened. He said he would like to come. We could hardly believe it. Evening came and we set off in two cars, Heather Alan and family, Barrie and I, Mum Dad and George, we filled a row. The chairs were arranged in a curve under the dome around the front of a semi- circular platform. This shape allowed for the audience or congregation to feel part of what was happening on stage, rather like a well-designed theatre. That night Dr Tony Stone, Vic Ramsey and an American guest speaker, Dave King were ministering to a packed room. They were working on words of knowledge, information that Holy Spirit was giving them. The first word was for a young man with a small lump behind his left ear. They called him to come to the front saying:

The Lord knows that this is just a small thing, but He wants to remove it, to show you how much He loves you.

Nothing happened, no one responded. I was so nervous thinking:

Oh God, all this time we have been praying for dad and we have finally got him to come and is this a hoax?

Although it is important to be able to wisely assess a situation, I realised that I had not given these people a chance and was too quick to judge negatively. With those thoughts pushed out of the way, one of the speakers turned round on the platform to face the area we were sitting, three rows back. He pointed saying:

There is a man sitting somewhere over here who is in his 50s, who has a long-standing back injury and has just been told he will never work again.

He also gave several other details. We all held our breath thinking the same thing that this has got to be dad, but will he respond? To our amazement he got up and walked to the front and stood just Infront of the platform and the microphones. They prayed for dad and then asked him to do something that he had been unable to do. So, despite the tight corset from his armpits to his hips, he bent over and got to about 6 inches from his toes. Over the microphones came dad's voice:

The pains gone. The pains gone!

Our row erupted as we jumped up and down, cried and praised God. Oh, how wonderful You are dear Lord. I feel quite emotional even now when I recall that night. At the end of the meeting a young man came forward. He apologised for being embarrassed and slow to come forward and then testified that the Lord had removed a lump from behind his left ear. I was so pleased the young man gained the courage to do that, so we were not left in any doubt about what happened.

Following the meeting we went back to Heather and Alans for a night cap. Dad wanted to test out his healing. He wanting to know if it had really happened, so he decided to give my nephew, a well-built 12-year-old a fireman's lift, up and down the stairs. The following day he was playing badminton over the washing line with the kids. Sunday came and we went swimming at Clipstone open air lido. It was a colliery facility and had two pools one for adults and a shallow one for the little people. Dad decided he was going to dive in and so he did several times. The joy on his face said it all. Monday, he rolled up his corset and threw it in the dustbin. Sometime between the Monday and the Saturday he was born again.

Having returned to Hull, dad went shopping on Holderness Road. It is a really long street lined with shops where you could buy anything that you needed really cheaply. There was a guy giving out Christian tracts at the side of the road to the shoppers, and passers-by. Normally Dad would have crossed the road to avoid people doing this sort of thing but he went up to him and asked if he had any of those things spare. The man asked him why he wanted them, and dad briefly told him his story and walked away with a fist full of tracts. My dad, the sceptical one who said leave me out of it, went along Holderness Road giving out tracts and telling any who would listen that God had healed him. Just how many miracles Dad had experienced I don't know but this was surely another big one. He did go back to work and retired around 65.

6

Reaching Out

About the same time that the adult group started in Alan and Heather's home, Tina's brother asked us if we could help him set up a youth group. There was nothing in the area for the young people of the church and as we had a good-sized lounge, could they use our home? We are not sure how it happened but unexpectedly after the first meeting we were left on our own with this wonderful group of young people. Our two nieces, our nephew and some of their friends were part of this group and slowly they all came to know Jesus. Using a neighbour's Bedford van, we took the group all over the area to take services, perform dramas, sing and play their instruments. It was a lovely time. One young man, the son of a local vicar, shared so much with his dad that one night his dad visited us seeking the baptism in Holy Spirit.[5] He drove home speaking in his spiritual language, known as speaking in Tongues in the Bible[5]. (This is a God given language that the speaker had not previously known). Not knowing how to stop the flow of this wonderful language, he sat in his car for a while and then he thought, all prayers end with Amen, so he said it out loud and then went into the vicarage.

Another a young man's parents were very anti anything Christian and made life very difficult for him, but he was steadfast and very courageous. He followed his call, went to college, and became an Anglican vicar. Years down the road, after this young man had got his first parish, he contacted us again. It was lovely to have the opportunity to catch up on all his news and witness just how the Lord had led him and taken care of him. He, along with all the other young people, had prayed for the sick and shared the gospel. They had written their own plays and were well able to work together to lead youth groups and services. What a joy and preparation for what God had instore for them.

We felt at one point that the Lord was prompting us to show the film, The Cross and Switchblade, in the local secondary school. So, a group of us got together to pray and with the school's permission, it went ahead. Thirty young people got born again that night. It says in Bible that angels rejoice over one person accepting Jesus, so they had plenty to rejoice over that night[8].

We really wanted to reach our neighbours in the village with the good news. We hit on the idea of inviting them along with other friends for an evening buffet once month and to ask a Christian speaker to come and share. This was a real success. In this informal setting, people felt free to ask questions and talk around the subjects presented. One evening we invited a missionary who had been out in Uganda. She was secretary to Bishop

Janani Luwum who was martyred in 1977 by Idi Amin. He wrote the book 'I love Idi Amin'. Unfolding a very moving story she shared that the bishop was able to love the sinner but not the sin. She acknowledged that she struggled with that, as just about every family had lost someone because of the evil this man committed.

Have you ever said something and instantly wished you hadn't? I can remember talking to the neighbour sitting next to me and saying:

I think I know enough about the Lord now to be able to forgive!

As the words left my mouth, I felt the 'OOCH' and regretted having said it?

A few days later a guy, that Barrie had put himself out to help, came round and verbally laid into Barrie. We were in the kitchen at the time, and I could feel myself getting angry with this man. How dare he, after everything Barrie had done for him. I could feel my foot really wanting to swing out at his ankle. Fortunately, Barrie could see what was going on in me and ushered me into the hall and shut the door. In that place the Lord reminded me of what I had said about forgiveness and I was struck with the emptiness of my own words and my pride. Good time to repent I thought. This was a very important lesson I was beginning to learn. I was impressed by how gracious Barrie was and with the Lord's help he poured oil onto those troubled waters.

Barrie and I could not get enough of Christian books and tapes. Our appetite was insatiable. This was a time to begin searching the Scriptures. We wanted to delve into the historical and cultural backgrounds, and subjects we had not previously considered. A time to find out what we really thought about issues and to face our doubts with honesty. To look at the challenges that traditional scriptural interpretation presents and consider the interface between our intellect and our faith. It was not enough to accept something just because a certain teacher, denomination or organisation said so. We wanted to know for ourselves. So, we learnt from a diverse group of teachers and writers e.g., David Pawson, Derek Prince, Alan Redpath, RT Kendal, John Stott, Watch Man Nee and so many more. But head knowledge is one thing, the practical out working, as you can see from the above story, is another.

We were sitting in St Swithin's one night after evensong and sitting behind us were Mr and Mrs Natick. Mr Natick owned a shop in the next village, but he had just been diagnosed as having cancer of the oesophagus. He was never a big man but he had lost a lot of weight due to his illness. We turned to talk to them and told them about some local healing meetings. We offered to take them if they wanted to go, however the last opportunity to attend was the evening of the following day. They said they were willing to give it a try so, the following evening we picked them up. God was again giving those ministering, words of knowledge[6] for people with certain illnesses to come and receive prayer. Unfortunately, Mr Natick's condition was not mentioned. We were very disappointed but not to be deterred we went forward with him anyway and asked for prayer. Nothing appeared to be happening for him at that point. But the next day he walked up the hill to our bungalow with a tray of eggs for us. The gates were closed to keep the children away from the road. He only had one hand free and that made opening the double gates difficult. So, balancing the tray of eggs in one hand he put his other hand on the gate and vaulted over with eggs still intact. He told us that when he got home after the meeting, he thought he would try things out. Swallowing had been difficult, so he tried a sausage roll and then cheese and biscuits. He had a full English breakfast that morning, before leaving the house. Over the next six weeks he ate everything he had not been able to previously and began to put on weight.

We are not sure what happened after that, but he began to deteriorate and became quite ill. I could not work it out. I was in a state of confusion and did not know what to say to them. Barrie continued to visit regularly, and they would read the Scriptures together. Mr Natick was at peace and died a few months later knowing his Saviour. Somethings remain a mystery.

I was so disappointed for them and even more so with myself for not visiting during Mr Natick's last days.

I asked God to forgive and strengthen me; so that If others needed help, I would be able to support them. Knowing God forgives is a wonderful release but there are times when we also need to forgive ourselves. That is sometimes the hardest thing to do. It may seem easier to forgive others, but it is just as important to stop beating ourselves up and forgive ourselves as God forgives us. We can then move on.

Those in the village who wanted to keep their business private but who needed prayer either for themselves, family or friends would visit us at night. Under the cover of darkness, they would walk up the hill and knock on our door. These events reminded us of Nicodemus in the Bible, you can read about him in John's Gospel chapter 3[7]. He visited Jesus at night because he also did not want to be seen. These events often surprised us, but we felt privileged to be asked to pray.

One man who had left the village and moved down south wrote to us to ask for prayer. He had been diagnosed as having terminal cancer and was obviously frightened of dying. This was another surprise, as he and his wife had been particularly critical about us and our faith. What a prayer opportunity that was! We were then able to pray, write back and send our love.

An older couple, Mr and Mrs Merridew lived in a bungalow down our road. They became adopted Grandma and Granddad to our children as our parents were in Hull. Mrs Merridew was an amazing cook. The chocolate buns and the scones she made were out of this world. One day just after Easter Mr Merridew wanted to talk about the doubts he had regarding God.

He was questioning, why was Jesus' death so special? Why was it any different to those, he had fought with in the war. Those who had given their lives on the battlefield on our behalf. This was a good question but at that time I did not have an answer for him but said that I would pray about it. Not long after this it was on the news about a child who had been killed by two other youngsters and the details were horrendous. I felt physically sick to the core and wondered how any adult could even think of doing those things, let alone youngsters. I felt like the Lord spoke to me like this:

You feel sick looking at this one terrible event, but I carried every terrible sin, from every nation, though all generations on myself on the cross. Can you imagine what that felt like?

Suddenly, the penny dropped, and I was over awed with the enormity of His sacrifice of love. This was the answer I had ask God for. At the next opportunity, I shared what I felt God had shown me with Mr Merridew and I think it helped him also.

One Saturday afternoon a couple arrived on our doorstep from Sheffield. I think they had got hold of our address from mutual friends. They were having marriage problems and were in quite a state, the wife especially. We sat down with them and listened to quite a complicated story. At the end of a rather long session with much prayer, we did not feel that we could help them further. We felt very sad and frustrated. They needed someone much nearer their home and we could not even recommend a referral as we did not know what help was available in their area. It was following this event and others that followed, that I began to realise that I needed to learn much more about Christian counselling but that was for a later time.

7

The Summer Camps

Early on in our Christian walk we were told about some Christian holiday camps. They were run by ' Good News Crusade' headed up by Don and Heather Double, Mike Dawood and the team. They also invited guest speakers from different nations. The first camps were at Chadacre, a place near Burry St Edmonds. It was an agricultural college but was hired out in the summer holidays. This sounded wonderful and there were also facilities for children and young people. Camping was free but there was an offering to cover their costs. For a young family with only one income, this sounded good.

We borrowed a neighbour's caravan and set off on a real adventure with Helen our first born who was four and Kate who was about six months old. The camp site was really well run by the site manager Jim. We camped in groups of around a hundred, in a circle like the old cowboy films. The people in charge of our unit were an Anglican vicar and his wife from West Wickham, with whom we became great friends. Here also, like at Kellam Hall, we saw some amazing miracles. People were receiving their sight, their hearing, short limbs were growing and so much more. We also became aware of the emotional healing that was going on and the deliverance from fears, the occult and addictions. What an eye opener to the love of God and the demonstration of His power.

One year we took several of our young people to the camp. One young lady, who became part of the youth group, had very bad eyesight. She wore glasses with bottle bottom lenses. She was a pretty, blond-haired young woman, but the glasses did not do much to reveal her attractiveness. During a time of worship her sight became blurred so, she removed her glasses to rub her eyes and found that she could see clearly without them. Another miracle. During the week she crumpled her glasses up and gave them to us as a reminder of her miracle. The faith of our young friends was inspiring, and we were all learning together.

The unit leaders were asked to recommend any people on their unit who could act as leaders or counsellors the following year. Our names were put forward to serve as counsellors. Gosh, this threw us into a panic, what should we do, did we know enough? These and many other questions came flooding into our minds. Eventually after some prayer and a whole load of anxiety, we decided that if we wanted to learn perhaps the hands-on approach was the next step, so we said yes.

The following year we served as counsellors on two camps, Chadacre and Braithwaite in Cumbria.

At the first camp, fear took over. What if people ask me stuff that I have no answer for? It was so bad that I hid in the caravan. I drew the curtains and shut the door to make it look like there was no one in.

A persistent caller came.

She knocked on the door and kept knocking until, out of shame, I answered it and invited her in. I just sat and listened to her and prayed but I did not have anything to give her that made sense. I felt useless but it caused me to go back to God many times during the year that followed, until I heard Holy Spirit's answer[6]. So now what? What do I do with Holy Spirit's answer? I did not have this lady's address and no guarantee that I would ever see her again. Perhaps it is too late I thought, but God had other ideas. At another camp a couple of years down the road, I caught a glimpse of her from a distance and ran to try and catch her. Rather out of breath I panted:

Do you remember me?

Yes: she said.

I went on to tell her what the Lord had revealed, and she cried. We prayed together in the middle of the crowd; it did not seem to matter that there were people looking on. God is so faithful; He knew my struggle and my heart and made the way for both her and myself, to meet again.

At that first camp, after feeling so inadequate I did get a break-through. I felt the Lord impress on me that I did not need to have all the answers. All He wanted me to do was love people. He would do the rest. He was the miracle worker, not me. He was the One with wisdom, not me. Oh, the relief of knowing He just wanted me to reach out in love, it somehow made it possible and dispelled the fear.

It was at the second camp that we witnessed and were part of a most moving miracle. On our unit there was a contingent from a church in Scotland and amongst them there was a family whose young daughter had cerebral palsy. She was unable to walk unsupported and needed a wheelchair to get around. This camp was on a hill side and the week was exceptionally wet. The paths were a sea of slippery mud which made them difficult to negotiate and remain upright. This situation made it impossible for her to use the wheelchair and more difficult for this young girl to be carried. One night after the evening meeting where many had been healed following words of knowledge[6], we were gathered in the centre of our unit for soup and fellowship. Norman, who was leading the unit asked if anyone had been disappointed that there had not been a word of knowledge for them? This young girl, supported either side by two strong men from their group said:

Yes, me.

Norman pointed out that it was the same God out here in our unit as it was in the big tent. He asked for those who had the faith to pray for her healing to gather round. Well, we had only just begun to pray when she pushed her supporters away and she ran and ran around the unit until she was out of breath. She stopped for a minute or so and started to run again just for the sheer joy of running. God had done it, both legs were healed, strong and whole, and both arms normal. We were all crying, not for sadness but for joy. Her family, members of her church and the those on the unit were there to witness this wonderful miracle. This young girl who had been unable to take part with the other young people, was now able to go out unassisted to be with her peers. A very different young girl returned home to Scotland with a powerful testimony.

A very different but wonderful miracle happened to a very tall, strong, retired R.E.M.Y. army sergeant. We were again at Braithwaite but this time as unit leaders. This couple and their two children had come to the camp because it was free not because it was Christian. In conversation one afternoon Barrie asked Rob, if he would like God to do anything for him whilst he was at camp? His reply surprised us, as this hunk of a man said he really wanted to cry! He went on to tell us that as a boy he had been told that men don't cry, as an army sergeant it was unacceptable for men to cry. So, when his dad died, although he wanted to show some emotion, he was unable to do so. Since that time, he had felt guilty that he was unable to show how much he loved his dad, by releasing tears. Well, we had never prayed a prayer like that for anyone before. When God released him, this great figure of a man erupted with tears and laughter alternately for quite a time, with no embarrassment but much relief. At last, he felt connected to who he was and at last at peace. The entire family got born again that week and went on to serve God in different ways. Rob and his wife ran a Christian bookshop for several years before going to China as missionaries. It is so wonderful to be part of God's amazing plans.

There are so many miracles we could share, but here is one that involved forgiveness. At one very wet camp, our lovely third daughter Erica (a cute curly haired three-year-old) at the time, got into mischief. The children used to play in the centre of the unit but because the grass was so wet, she had managed to get into a tent belonging to someone else. Whilst she was in there, she discovered some cornflour and lard and decided to do some mixing. She had found a bowl but somehow manged to spread it much further than the receptacle. She had covered a large swathe of the tent with this greasy concoction and herself into the bargain. The first we knew about it was when this dear forgiving couple walked her across the unit to our tent. She looked like a small snow man covered in flour and if this was the state she was in, what condition was their tent in? Children have the habit of keeping you humble!

Every camp had its own theme. One memorable year at Chadacre the camp theme was, Holiness unto the Lord. By the Wednesday people had experienced healings, deliverances and many were released into a new freedom to enjoy life. That evening at 7pm when we gathered in the big top. Something felt different. Instead of music, there was silence. No one spoke and the tent was being filled with a mist that radiated light. The Shekinah Glory descended from the top of the tent and we either sat or lay prostrate on the ground. No one ministered, they could not and did not even try. About ten o clock people began to move ever so quietly and go back to their tents. The camp was silent but surprisingly the Glory was outside the big top and all over the camp site. The air particles where radiating light. We did not need a torch, not even in our own tents. Barrie and I quietly got ready and went to bed. That night the police were receiving calls from local residents in the area, complaining about the music that was being played into the early hours, coming from the camp. People on the camp were woken up by the music and singing but the camp lay silent. It was the angelic hosts praising God that they were hearing. Barrie and I slept through it and I felt a little disappointed that we had missed that but so grateful that we had been in the Shekinah Glory. That was something we will never forget.

8

No Ordinary Family Life

Whilst Barrie was doing his teacher training, our only income was Barrie's bursary. It was not much for a family to manage on, so we did not have any money to buy the oil for our central heating boiler. The winter was fast approaching. We did, however, have an open fire in the lounge. Quite a few of our neighbours worked for the colliery and received a monthly allowance of coal. We never asked, but bags of coal would appear outside our back door. We were never without an open fire all though the cold weather. God is so good. It was not only our neighbours in the village who looked out for us, but also those in the next village

Tina's brother Jim and family had a farm in Ompton. It was the next village going out towards Newark. We had asked him if he had any spare manure for our garden and he answered:

Yes, sure I will drop you some off.

We were getting ready to go to a wedding one Saturday. We had dressed Helen in her best clothes. We were in our best bib and tuckers and just about to get into the car to go when the phone rang. It was Jim:

I'm on the way now.

We replied: Jim we are just going to a wedding. We are in our best clothes, well!

Jim: It's ok, I have the manure in the trailer and it tips.

Not long after, we could hear the tractor engine as it was coming down the road and then it appeared around the bend. You should have seen the size of that trailer! The manure once tipped filled the two to three car parking area at the front of our house. Once the job was done, we thanked Jim and had to leave this smelly mountain to drive to the wedding in Mansfield.

The day after the wedding, it rained and rained some more, thoroughly soaking our mountain of manure. The rainwater filtered through the manure and ran down the gutter past the houses on our road, down the hill and into the village. Now, not everyone likes the smell of manure and not everyone wants a river of it running outside their house. We started to wonder if this was such a good idea after all. It was going to take weeks to wheelbarrow it up into our back garden, there was so much of it. Then the idea struck us. We could ask the neighbours to come and take a barrow load for their gardens. That might off set the inconvenience caused and also help to whittle down the pile. It still took weeks to get the car park cleared but at least we had shared the blessing and the village gutters were the most fertile in Britain!

It was not only manure that ended up on our front garden. One morning we woke up to loud Mooing. Cows belonging to a local farmer had somehow got out of their field and decided to have an early morning stroll down the road towards the village. They took a slight detour as they had seen tasty vegetation in one of the well manured gardens . . . Ours. I don't know how many were availing themselves of our tasty delights, but the garden looked full. It was funny, but dangerous at the same time because of the blind bend. These cows were huge and very heavy. The lawn could testify to that. There was a frantic ringing round until the right farmer was located and he came with his farm hands to get them to safety. Relief, both the cows and traffic were now safe.

Thinking about local farmers; we had made friends with several in the area. One farmer who lived by the cricket green would give us a call when his pigs or sheep had their young and we would take the girls to see them. There was also a little biscuit treat for the girls to nibble on the way home. One farmer near Rufford Park had goats and as Helen was allergic to cows' milk, he would give us ring and we could go and pick up a bottle or two of goat's milk.

There was a ford on the back road to Rufford Park, not far from Wellow and when it rained the water in the ford would rise considerably. It was great fun riding your bicycle through the water hoping you didn't catch your wheel on a stone. Falling off meant a cold wet ride home. One day an elderly friend from Mansfield came to visit. He decided that he would come via the back road which meant going through the ford at Rufford. That day some boys were standing on stones in the Ford and as Alfred approached in his rather posh BMW, the boys beckoned him through. They were so naughty. They had given the impression by standing on stones that the water was shallow and you've guessed it. He got stuck and water flooded into the car filling the seat wells and the engine stalled. The boys cashed in on this dilemma and for a small fee offered to push his car out of the ford. I don't know how much they made that day, but I bet it was substantial. Alfred had been well and truly conned and had to return home that day in a pair of Barrie's trousers, socks, and shoes.

We did not live far from the Major Oak in Sherwood forest, in 'Robin Hood Country'. Sometimes we would take the girls there for a walk and whilst there, we were told about something that had just occurred. Some American visitors had been sightseeing at the famous Oak. They had heard gun shots and terrified fell face down, spread eagle in the mud wondering what was happening (before you ask, no, it was not raining and muddy all the time). The army had a training camp really close by and they were out on manoeuvres when they got a bit too close to the civilian boarder. Our American friends thought they were under attack. They took the evasive action that left them looking like they were wearing army camouflage too – mud and lots of it. I bet they will never forget that experience, or the ruined clothes. The locals thought this highly amusing but in true British form, concealed their laughter at the time so as not to offend.

The girls wanted to learn how to ride a bicycle. One problem – we did not have any bikes that they could learn on. We were a one income family so to buy new bikes was out of our reach. We told the girls, if you want bikes you will have to pray as we don't have money to buy them. So, we all prayed and asked God if He would help us?

A couple of days later a friend in the village came round and asked if we wanted a bike? Their daughter had grown out of hers and needed a larger model. The first bike arrived and was just the right size for Helen. Someone in the next village was getting rid of their children's bikes for the same reason. They asked us if we knew of anyone who needed them before they got taken to the tip. Two more bikes arrived. Kate and Erica were now the proud owners of their own two wheels. We thought that's it, job done, thank You Lord, but the bikes kept coming. We were now giving them away. Eventually we had to say to the girls that we needed to pray again and ask God to stop sending them. This done no more bikes arrived but what a miracle for the girls to witness. God loves them so much that He was willing to help out, even with things that were not a necessity.

People have asked us several times over the years, what we considered the most important thing to teach your children? We have always answered:

Teach them to pray and hear God for themselves, because as parents we cannot be with them all the time, in every situation, but God can. He is there, able to care for them even when we are out of reach.

Did we as parents get everything right? No of course we didn't. Learning by our mistakes has also been a significant part of family life. If we never get anything wrong, we wouldn't need to learn about forgiveness or perseverance. How are our children going to learn these things if we don't demonstrate them? Asking for and receiving forgiveness are valuable lessons for life. Being humble enough to admit when we have missed the mark and try again, opens the way for our children to follow.

As there wasn't a school in the village the children had to catch the school bus. It picked them up on the village green and took them to the next village, Ollerton, where there were both primary and secondary schools. This all sounds fairly simple but it was traumatic for our eldest, because unbeknown to us she was bullied on the bus and consequently hated the journey. Eventually we caught on and with a little intervention, the situation improved. On Wednesdays, my sister who had a car would come and pick me up so I could meet Helen, Kate and Erica at school, and we would go to Heather's for tea before returning home. The teachers knew that on Wednesdays I would be there, so any information that was required would be passed on then. The information included anything that the children had done wrong or needed to improve upon. It was not always comfortable. One particular day, a rather irate teacher was waiting for me and this is how it went.

Teacher: Mrs Lucas you really must be more specific with your children.

Me: Why what do you mean?

Teacher: I asked Kate, is mummy coming to pick you up today?

Kate answered: I don't know.

Teacher: So, I said to her, what exactly did mummy say?

Kate replied that mummy said: She would come God willing, and I don't know if He is?

Teacher: So, you see you must be more specific. We have all been standing here waiting for a sign from heaven to tell us if God is willing or not!

Well, she was obviously really cross with me so after apologising and promising to do better, Kate and I made a speedy exit.

Esther, our fourth child was born in 1980. She was a cheeky blond haired, blue eyed beauty. The girls loved her and encouraged her into all sorts of scrapes, but she has survived to tell the tail. When she was about one, we had a call from the pastor of an Elim church in Norwich.

He had had contact with a group of believing, born again Gypsies (as they were called at that time). This group were wanting to come to Nottinghamshire and were looking for a site to be able to park their caravans. Apparently, some sites were exclusive and not open to other groups. His question was, did we know where they could stay? We knew of a local site in the next village so said we would make enquires. The next day I was going to put Esther in the seat on the back of my bicycle to ride down to the Gypsy camp, but I could not find her reigns. I needed them to strap her safely in the seat. Nor could I find my bicycle clips so what was I going to do? I did find some string so, making use of that I tied it around my trouser legs, and then tied Esther into her seat! We must have looked quite a sight but off we went. When we arrived at the camp site, we stopped on the side of the road. We were greeted by some very noisy and aggressive geese with necks outstretched ready to attack. A tethered dog was barking loudly nearby and straining on its lead. I was worried and did not want to put Esther at risk from these fierce animals but fortunately a man came out to see what all the noise was about. I told him what I wanted, and he invited us round to the door of his caravan to give me the information I needed, as this site was not an open one. In His caravan, I could see from the door that, there was someone in the bed at the end. He told me that his mother had had an operation and was not recovering from it. He was obviously very concerned.

I asked if I could pray for her and he said yes. So, with Esther tucked under my arm we went in and prayed for this old lady. Then we thanked him and left after tying Esther back into her seat. It might sound like quite an easy task riding your bicycle with a child on the back, but Esther liked to sing. With her singing, she would sway from side to side – you get the picture.

We passed the relevant information on to our friend in Norwich and got an update of where and when his travelling people were headed. That done I thought I would let the man on the local camp know. Esther and I cycled back to the gypsy camp. This time I had found the reins and my cycle clips, so we looked in better shape. The man came out as before and seemed really pleased to see us. He said that his mother would like to meet us. We dismounted and went round to his caravan. His mother was up and wanted to thank us for praying. She had started to get better just after we had prayed and wondered if we had any Bibles, we could give them. I had been told that not many of the older people could read, but the younger ones could read to them all. So, we delivered several Bibles in modern language.

Sometime later we had a visit from a Gypsy caravan train who parked rather precariously down the road into the village. There were quite a few of them but they called just to say thank you. God is so good, and this prompted quite a few conversations with curious neighbours.

I mentioned earlier that we lived last but one going out of the village and then there was the blind bend which could be quite dangerous. One day I was cleaning in the hallway when I heard a very loud bang. I looked out of the lounge window to see what was going on. There had been a nasty collision of a car with a large van. The car had come to a halt on the verge outside of Tina's bungalow and the van was on the other side of the road facing towards the village. I could see that the car was badly damaged. First thing I did was drop to my knees and quickly pray, the next I rang for an ambulance, the fire brigade, and the police. Then I ran down the drive straight to the car. There were a man and a woman in this vehicle that had been concertinaed from side to side. The window was smashed on the passenger side and I was able to talk to them. The lady's arm was obviously broken, and they were both in a lot of pain. I told them that help was on the way. She was distraught and told me that she was pregnant and really worried about her baby. I told them that I was a Christian and believed in miracles and asked them if I could pray for them. They seemed willing, so that is what I did. Not too long after help arrived, and I stayed with them until they had been cut free from the car and transferred to the ambulance. The police were taking down details from the man in the van who was shaken but on his feet. They also looked after the traffic on the blind bend. A few days later I manage to get through to the ward where the lady was taken and found out that she was doing ok. What is in a morning? I had no idea what was going to happen that day when I awoke but I was glad that God knew.

A couple of months later this couple came back to tell me all was ok and baby alive and kicking. They also wanted to thank me for the help and the prayers. It was lovely to know, that with the burden to pray, also came the answers.

Barrie tells the next story.

I was teaching fulltime at a school in Derbyshire in a town named Shirebrook, but we were living in Nottinghamshire. Consequently, I needed a car to get to work. This story starts just before the summer holidays in the late 70s. Our mini clubman estate had gone twice round the clock on the mileometer. I had made friends with the local mechanic at the garage. We had arranged that when the car was due for its MOT, I would take it to him a few weeks prior and he would give it the once over. He would then tell me what was needed to be done for it to pass. Then he would give me the option of doing the repairs myself or paying him to do them. This time he said that the amount of work needed was excessive and would cost more than the car was worth. This was bad news as we did not have the money to replace the car. Nina and I prayed. We needed help and help came from an unexpected source.

A friend Will and his wife from across the village, had taken on the franchise for the local post office. He rang me one evening and the conversation went something like this –

Will: You have the summer holidays coming up and you are practical, aren't you?

I answered yes.

Will went on to say: I had intended to refit our kitchen and have bought all the units and fittings. But now that I have taken on the post office, I have not got the time to do the work. Would you be willing to do it for me and I will pay you?

The first thought that went through my head was, 'Lord You are amazing'. We had only just prayed about financing a replacement car. Of course, I said yes. I spent four weeks of the summer holiday stripping out the old kitchen, fitting plumbing and electrics, plastering, fitting the new units, wall and floor tiles and finally painting. Will was so pleased with all this work and asked what he owed me. I said that I would go home and put the bill together. I needed to include the extra parts and materials I had bought, and the number of hours worked to make up an invoice. Having done so, I felt I should pray and ask God if I was charging the right amount and felt the Lord say, No. I asked the question, what should I charge then? And sensed the Lord said' I want you to give it to him'. This was not the response I either wanted or expected. With the need of a new car at the front of my thoughts, I set off with the invoice in my pocket.

Will said: How much do I owe you?'

As my hand went to reach for the invoice, out of my mouth came:

Nothing, I am giving it to you!

Will was speechless and so was I. He just could not believe that I could do that. To be honest neither could I. On the way home I was thinking that I was the biggest idiot out and to cap it all my brother-in-law had parked his posh Humber Sceptre (with overdrive) Infront of our house. I went in and the first thing Alan said was:

Have you sorted a replacement car yet?

Embarrassed, I said: No.

Alan replied: Well, you have now. I am buying a new car and asked the Lord if I should trade my car in or sell it privately and felt the Lord say neither, I want you to give it to Barrie!

The car Alan had just given me was worth more than double what I would have charged for doing the kitchen. How good is that? We were learning that when you are doing what God asks, it is impossible to out give Him. God was showing us something of His great provision.

In 1981 we felt that the Lord was calling us to get ready for a move. At that point we had no idea where to, a bit like Abraham or even St Columba. Part of the preparation was to put our house on the market. You may have prayed prayers like, 'Lord everything I have is Yours', well we had too. However, it is only when it is put to the test you find out if your possessions are really His or not. This was our first home as a family, and we had done so many things to make it our own. Barrie had built a garage and outside store and supporting garden walls. He had learned about brick laying. I had made curtains and learned about gardening, painting and decorating. We had brought the children up from babies here with so many memories. We had so many friends and neighbours. We had seen so many miracles. So, who's 'house' was it?

We prayed again, acknowledging that although our prayers had been well intended, they lacked any depth of understanding, so we committed ourselves again to God's will and purpose.

The house was on the market for two years before it sold. By that time, we were sure that God wanted us to go to Shrewsbury, Shropshire. We had met two pastors from that town whilst on the Good News Crusade camps. One of the pastors recently had a death in his family. He was looking for someone to visit his bereaved relative who lived not too far from our home in Wellow. On the last day of a camp preparation weekend, we were sitting on the same table as these Pastors. I think we were the answer to the pastor's prayers and had the privilege of visiting his relative until we knew she was going to be ok. This was just the start of many relationships . . .

As Barrie has mentioned, had been working in a town named Shirebrook in Derbyshire. It was a town that had experienced a lot of division. Three communities of miners had been thrown together. As pits closed in Poland and Wales, these two groups and their families moved to Shirebrook. This caused no end of friction and rivalry often resulting in violence. One evening whilst Barrie was waiting to teach a night class – for a bit of exercise he went out for a walk. He stopped to look in a shop window in the town and became aware of a group of youths behind him. They were coming towards him and he could hear comments like, Let's get him. They started to run at him. Barrie instead of running turned to face them. As he turned and looked into their eyes, the three of them stopped in their tracts. They looked at each other and turned and walked away. Barrie thought that they had probably expected him to run and perhaps wondered if he was able to defend himself, either way God kept him safe. The threat disappeared.

The head of the CDT (Craft Design and Technology) department where Barrie worked, did not want him to move. He was not an easy man to get on with, but Barrie was able to relate to him and he valued Barrie's support. So, for several reasons he tried his best to persuade him to stay. He offered promotion and increments on his salary. He even offered to keep his job for him should things not work out for us in Shrewsbury, but God had called us and we wanted to follow.

The summer holidays were fast approaching, and we were about to move. Our house was sold, and Barrie had submitted his resignation. Everything was set for us to work on the summer camps and then move to Shrewsbury when disaster struck. The sale of our house fell through.

We wondered, 'What do we do now?'

We were relying on this sale to finance a place to live in Shropshire. This was not the sort of news we wanted or expected. After all some people said, that if God was in something, it would all run smoothly.

So, 'where does that leave us?' we thought.

After much prayer, we did not feel that God had changed His mind. He is the same yesterday, today and forever, so that did not seem like His character. His purposes for us were still the same, so we decided to move regardless and trust Him with the details.

You might ask: What were His purposes?

Well, we felt that God wanted us to move to Shrewsbury to train us. At one point Barrie had felt that he should train for some sort of ministry, perhaps even the Church of England. Somehow nothing seemed quite right. We did not know just what form the training would take, but we had that quiet surety we recognised as faith, that this was the right thing to do. That assurance held us on course through many a storm.

PART 2

9

A Leap of Faith

Leaving a neighbour with a key and our nephew to cut our grass, we locked up our bungalow, furniture, and all, and set off for the camps. Moving away from the village, family and friends was a strange feeling. It was almost like removing a rather large, warm overcoat – a safety blanket, and at the same time having butterflies in the stomach. It was a mix of anxiety with excitement.

Like Abraham we had a large tent (an eight-birth). After working on the camps, we drove to Shrewsbury with our four lovely girls, a trailer, tent, camping equipment and a pile of dirty washing!

We arrived on the doorstep of the pastor, the one who's relative had been bereaved. He and his wife were expecting us, and we wondered what help they could offer. What we needed initially was a place to stay. He had two options; one of which was to pitch our tent on his lawn or to stay with a couple who had a large house on the outskirts of the town. We plumbed for tent and garden option. So, in true Abrahamic style, we pitched our tent there for six weeks, taking up the lion's share of their garden.

Barrie needed a job. As we were now living in Shrewsbury, he was able to register as a supply teacher at the Shire Hall. Initially there were no vacancies, and he did not want to register as unemployed. He felt that as God had led us there, He would provide him with work. Barrie believed that the subsequent revenue would be enough to cover the cost of living in Shrewsbury and pay the mortgage of the house in Wellow. There are so many stories of God's financial provision . . . But, first let me tell you about our accommodation:

As we were camping on the garden but also needed to use the toilet facilities in the house, Barrie and I slept on the lounge floor to enable the Pastor's back door to be kept open. That year there had been a plague of ants. On waking up in the morning we found an ant trail next to our airbed. Ahhhhh, not what I expected, and they are not easy to get rid of. So, we shared the space with God's little creatures for the duration of our stay.

One day the pastor's wife asked me if either we, or the children had eaten the salmon out of the fridge? I asked the children, and the answer was unanimously, No. Oh dear, this looked like we had stolen it. What alternative conclusion was there? Then a couple of days later the answer to prayer came. We spotted the neighbour's large tom cat pawing open the fridge door and nosing inside. But how did the cat get in unnoticed? Well, they had a flat roof over the front door, just below the open window of their son's bedroom. This rather daring animal had jumped on to the roof and got in through this window, made his way down the stairs and crept into the kitchen. What a cheek! But what a relief, as all suspicion was now gone.

We could see that having six other people share your garden and house was becoming a strain, but help was on the way. A family in the church wanted to borrow our camping equipment to go on holiday for two weeks and said that we could use their house whilst they were away. Would that be ok with us? No need to think about that one – it was another answer to prayer! Whilst we were enjoying the freedom of their home, a young woman came to see us. She asked us if we would look after her house as she was getting married and moving to London. She said she had put it on the market, and it was ours to use until it was sold. The timing could not have been better. It was a lovely three-bedroom semi-detached house not far from where we had been staying and it enabled the girls to continue at the local school. One drawback however was, this lovely lady was a music teacher and in her lounge was the most beautiful Steinway piano. Our four young children found this a great attraction but with swinging feet and careless hands, it was an expensive accident waiting to happen. The owner kindly had it moved as soon as she could.

Kate was normally a very calm and balanced little girl but one day not long after we had moved into this home, she was uncontrollable. Nothing we said or did made any difference. We just did not know what to do so, Barrie and I shut the door of our bedroom to pray.

It only seemed to take a few minutes before I could see a flash back of an occasion in our home in Wellow. I was standing on the landing shouting angrily at Kate, almost out of control. I do not recall why but I felt the Lord showing me that Kate had somehow imbibed my anger and that because of all the changes we were going through, it had surfaced. I realised that I needed to repent and ask the Lord's forgiveness, then explain to Kate and ask for her forgiveness. This I did and we never had a reoccurrence of that type of attack.

It was whilst we were in this property our Niece, Sharon from Nottinghamshire visited us with her friend. Sharon met a lovely young man named Keith from the Shrewsbury fellowship and a flame was ignited. They fell in love and a couple of years later got married. I just love a romance. Communications between the two areas were becoming established. We arranged visits between the Youth fellowship that had met in our Wellow home and the young people from this Baptist church. My sister Heather and my brother-in-law Alan, also visited and they eventually moved to Shrewsbury eighteen months later with Sharon's younger brother and sister.

Around this time, we came into-contact with a lady we had met whilst shopping in the town. This lady had been on an excess of drugs for her mental health condition. Her psychiatrist had tried to reduce her drug intake and it had a dramatic effect. She laid down in front of a bus in the town, thinking that it was a refreshing pool of water she could bathe in. Consequently, she was sectioned for a while. One day, in a very dirty condition she came to see us. Esther was aged 2 at the time and would not go near her. We realised that there was something very spiritually wrong as Esther was a very friendly little girl. This behaviour was out of character for her. It transpired that this lady, in her weak and vulnerable condition, had joined a local witches coven. We were not unfamiliar with this type of situation, as we had had contact with others struggling to break free from both covens and Satan's temple in Nottinghamshire.

She had not attended the coven gathering for a while so coven members were following her around. Looking out of our window we could see a car, parked outside. She recognised it as belonging to one of the witches. She did not want to leave the house as she was frightened. She did not know what they might do to her. She knew there were penalties for disobedience. After a time, they would drive off, but this happened on quite a few occasions.

We had opportunity to pray with and for her, and God began to set her free from demonic oppression. Esther began to get a little bit closer to her and eventually climbed on her knee. This lady began to smell a lot sweeter and dress in clean clothes. With the help of the Lord and an excellent psychiatrist, she also got free from the drugs she was taking. She moved into a nice little flat and managed to hold down a job. She was also reunited

with her estranged children and years later, passed on to
be with her Saviour.

To go back a little; there were other houses up for
sale on this estate where we were living that seemed
to sell quickly, but this one remained on the market for
six months and provided a lovely home for us. When
it eventually sold, we spent a couple of weeks with a
couple in a nearby village. Then an older couple who had
a large home at the other side of the Quarry (a large park
in the centre of Shrewsbury) offered us accommodation.
This was such a sacrifice for them. They had been used
to their own quiet space and a family of six was about to
shatter that. They helped us in no end of ways but not
wanting to get under their feet I walked the children
across Shrewsbury to school. I set off quite early and
walked little Esther around for hours in her buggy. Then
we would walk all the way back. One of the good things
about it was that we all kept fit, and the children slept
exceptionally well at nights.

It was also an anxious time, as we did not know
what the future held or where we would end up. I must
admit, that even if people thought we were strong,
I was struggling. I had bad tooth ache and made an
appointment with the dentist. After examining my
teeth, he asked if I was under any stress? I said yes and
mentioned our situation of having been of 'no fixed
abode' for nearly a year with four children. He said that
there was nothing wrong with my teeth, but my all my

nerves where jangling. He recommended a tooth paste for sensitive teeth and to come back if the nerves did not settle down.

We were learning so many things just not the training we thought we were going to receive. What comes to your mind when you think about training? For me it was something like school: Learning from books, mentoring and being shown practical demonstrations. Little did I know that God was teaching us how to receive. This was a humbling experience. In the normal run of things, we are both independent, confident, and practically able people, but we had to rely so much on other people and ask for everything e.g., may I bathe the children, or can I cook them a meal now? This meant that the pride we had held on to, regarding our independence, was taking a beating. It is not easy to learn about giving but we found that learning to receive was even harder.

Whilst we were with these dear people, our house in Wellow sold. What a relief! We began to look around for something to buy and saw many houses that were not suitable for a family of six. Eventually a friend from the church had seen one for sale 'Four Winds', on Belvidere walk. It was not far from the church, school, the Shire Hall, and a short walk into town. He insisted that we go and have a look. On first viewing we could see this older property needed so much doing to it. We felt we could not afford to buy it and still be able to pay for all the repairs, so we dismissed it. A week or two later this same friend asked if we had been to see it? We told him that it needed too much doing to it for it to be affordable. He insisted that we go and have another look.

On our second viewing, it was as if we could see past its condition to its potential and suddenly it became a contender. We had asked several friends around the country to pray for us and two people had sent descriptions of the house they had seen whilst in prayer. We looked at these two pictures and they were both different. That was confusing, but then we realised that one was the front and the other the side elevation of 'Four Winds'. That confirmed it and the deal was done.

We now needed to return to Wellow to collect our furniture. We set off with a hired van on a Friday afternoon and arrived at 'Columba Folk' in the evening. Keith, who was dating our niece Sharon, was keen to help and came with us. Because it was rather late when we arrived, we thought we would load up most of the things in the morning. The new owners were not due until after lunch on the Saturday or so we thought. Just as we were getting ready for bed another van pulled up on the drive. The new owners knocked on the door and were as surprised as we were. After a short chat we discovered that this young doctor and his wife were also Christians. We made up our sofa bed for them and we all had a good night's rest. How did that happen? It all seemed so ridiculous, but we now knew that the people living in our old home would pray and be a witness in that place.

First thing in the morning we loaded up our van quite quickly, as we had two more pairs of hands to help. We then helped the new family to unload their van before setting off back to Shropshire. Our furniture was distributed safely around the fellowship for people to store, until we could move into our new home.

10

God's Provision of Work

During that first year we witnessed God's provision of work first-hand. *Barrie* gives the story in his own words.

I did not feel that it was honourable to sign up as unemployed so I registered as self-employed trusting that I would be gainfully occupied. On our first Sunday in Shrewsbury, the pastor of the church announced that I was available for work and able to do most types of maintenance. God provided work for every day that I needed it, but I never had work planned for more than two or three days in advance. Some weekends there would be nothing booked for the following week but come the Monday morning, I would have at least the first day's work. One Sunday, Ann, a lady in the church approached me after the service and said:

I have just a little job I would like done. It will not take you all day so perhaps you could fit my job in between others.

I replied that I had nothing for Monday and would come then anyway.

I asked her: What is it you that you want doing?

She told me that her front door required a surrounding draft excluder fitting. I replied that I would be with her about 10am. Early Monday morning I visited the builder's merchant to buy the draft excluder kit. Having selected the kit, I was making my way to the cash point when I felt the Lord spoke to me. I am certain that I heard him say:

Buy Three.

It was at this point that I began to argue with Him. I thought I do not need three, I only need one. I felt he repeated:

I want you to buy three.

The kit was priced at £7. The contents of my wallet revealed I had exactly £21. My next thoughts were that if I buy three, I will have spent all the money I have and will have two kits that I don't need. I continued to walk towards the cash out with one kit and God's Holy Spirit asked:

Are you going to buy three or . . . ?

I realised that there was no point in arguing further. I went back and picked up two more. On the way back to the cash out, I thought to myself that if we ever get to buy a house here, I can fit one to our front door and one to the back.

When I arrived at Ann's and started to fit her draft excluder, I became aware of a gentleman standing nearby. He asked:

Can you fit me one of those, I live across the road?

I answered: Ok.

Whilst I am fitting the excluder for this man, a lady came and stood by me and asked if I could fit her one! She lived three doors down. What would have been only a couple of hours work that would hardly pay me for my time, became a full day's work and pay. Plus, I had used all three sets of draft excluders. This was another lesson, in not to argue with Holy Spirit.

During this first year I did some gardening, decorating, roof repairs, plumbing, manufacturing large portable mirrors for a dancing school, lamp design and manufacture, some ceramics, car servicing, electrical and safety checks. The jobs were numerous and varied.

We had two elderly ladies in the church who were 'born again' in the Welsh revival. They knew that they needed their electrical devices servicing. Being quite frail, they had been afraid to invite strangers into their home, however, they felt safe asking me, as someone they knew. It was indeed appropriate timing as several of their appliances had become unsafe. What a joy and a pleasure to be able to serve these faithful old saints.

A phone call from the education department came at the end of that year. New government education policy meant that all CDT teachers throughout Shropshire, would need to be retrained to deliver the new National Curriculum. As a result of this policy and that they could see from my CV that I was already trained in these subjects, I was suddenly in great demand. They needed me to cover whilst teachers were absent for retraining. I was sent to several schools in Shrewsbury and quite a few in Shropshire. This took up the best part of two years and as a result gave me access into many CDT departments in the county where I made numerous friends.

One of the schools that I was sent to as a supply teacher was Adams Grammar School in Newport. Whilst I was working in another school, Adams Grammar School contacted me and asked if I had seen the advertisement for the post of Head of CDT? Would I be interested in applying? I sent in the application and was successful. I taught there happily until I retired.

11

'Four Winds'

We did not know how we were going to pay for the extensive repairs that were needed but if God had spoken then He would supply.

When moving day arrived, people came to help from all over the area. They brought our furniture in vans, cars, and trailers. It must have looked like Steptoe and Son were moving in. The carpets had been cleaned and vacuumed the day before, so people were able to dust and put furniture into place. One person washed the windows at the front, another round the back. Someone else cut the grass. The cupboards were filled, and everything was in place with the beds made before 5pm. The children went mad. They ran in and out of every door, upstairs and down, just for the joy of having their own space. They explored the garden and made a little den, the first of several. Even though they got under people's feet, no one seemed to mind. They understood what it meant to the children to have their own home again. It was all so wonderful and at 7pm we were able to host guests for a simple meal! What a memorable day that was.

One night before we moved in, I had a dream in which I could see 'Four Winds', with white envelopes falling like confetti on the roof. What's all that about? After moving in, these white envelopes started to arrive. Some came via the postal service and some just pushed through the letter box with no address, only our names. All had gifts of money in them. Wow how faithful you are God. This money paid for all the extensive repairs e.g., a new kitchen, bathroom and toilet, new plumbing, and electrics, plastering and decoration. and then stopped coming.

Having a home of our own enabled us to have visitors again. We had not seen my Mum and Dad for what seemed like a long time, so a visit was planned. Barrie had renovated and repaired an old car that some friends had given him. They did not have the time or inclination to do the work so, they said that if he did it up, he could sell it and keep the money. Once done, he advertised it in the local paper which was published on a Friday. This weekend we were very excited waiting for mum and dad to arrive. We expected them to arrive around teatime and had everything ready. The doorbell rang, we all rushed to the front door, children hopping from one foot to the other with excitement and I was in playful mood. I lifted the flap on the letter box and began to sing,

Who's that knocking on my door,
Who's that knocking on my door,
Have you been this way before,
Who's that knocking on my door.

I opened the door to see two very surprised (perhaps in shock) young men. Falteringly they said that they had come about the car. I don't know what they must have thought, being serenaded through a letter box. I was so embarrassed, and the girls were doubled up with laughter. Since then, this occasion has been known as 'Mother and the singing letter box!' with other comments like – What will mother do next?

During our time in Nottinghamshire little Erica had been having trouble with ear infections. The consultant had recommended, that because of the recurring nature of this problem and the fluid in her ears, that she should have grommets fitted. These little tubes drain away the excess fluid. Unfortunately, by the time her operation date came through we were moving. This consultant said that they would transfer her notes etc once we were settled in our new location and registered with the hospital in Shrewsbury. That is what we did, and her notes were transferred to a local consultant. At the first appointment, the consultant examined Erica and we were all surprised. He could not find anything at all wrong! A miracle of healing had occurred sometime that year, in between leaving Nottinghamshire and moving into our new home. Thank you so much Lord.

12

God Takes Us at Our Word

When we were born again, we had said to the Lord that he could send who He liked to us but please would He keep the larder full. It seemed like He was taking us at our word but He also kept His. We not only had our parents and friends to stay, but God sent others.

The first visitors that came were a family of four. They had sold their house and the new house was not quite ready to move into. In order not to lose the sale of their old property, they needed somewhere to stay. It was late autumn and getting colder. Initially they lived in their caravan parked on our drive. But because of the cold weather and the increasing amounts of condensation, we suggested that they move into our house. Their children and ours had so much fun together and we shared the cooking and housework. I do not remember how many weeks we were together, but we built a friendship that has lasted to the present day.

Our next visitors were a lady and her daughter. We had met at school. She was experiencing marriage problems and felt she could not cope anymore. We converted our dining room into a bedroom as she needed her own space. Her daughter shared with our daughter Kate. They were with us for nearly a year and stayed until they were back on their feet. During that time the lady, who was formerly a Jehovah Witness, accepted Jesus as her Lord and Saviour. We were so pleased that she was eventually reconciled to her husband, and the family reunited.

A young woman who had been working as a nanny for a family in Shrewsbury became unemployed and subsequently without accommodation. The family she was with, moved away. She had been coming to our church and our girls got on well with her. You have guessed it, she moved in. She took orders for knitted garments and toys for a local business and spent hours teaching the girls to knit. She also had other part time jobs that gave her the extra finance she needed. Whilst she was with us, she met a young man and they eventually got married. For a few years they rented a cottage not far from our home, but they are now living in Leicestershire with their own family.

We led a wonderful house group that proved so much fun and gave us all opportunities to learn. Derek, a young man in this group had stayed with us when we were in Nottinghamshire whilst he did a course on Agricultural Engineering. I don't think he was prepared for an encounter with our four girls. One day when he returned from his course, we had a surprise for him. You can imagine the look of horror on his face when we confronted him with:

The girls have picked up hair lice from school!' Ug!

This meant that we all had to have our hair washed with the recommended shampoo. After washing the girl's hair thoroughly with this pungent lotion, it was Derek's turn. With his head over the side of the bath, he could not stop squirming from the thought that he might have picked up some of these little critters. Despite that shock we are still friends. This lovely young man married an equally lovely young woman who also came to our home group. He is now serving God as an Anglican vicar.

13

More than One Way of Learning

Despite the many events/adventures we had experienced, we still felt that God wanted to train us. Apart from learning how to receive, we needed to learn more about other things that are not learnt from a book. For example, how to deal with rejection and how to love people despite the things they may do – we needed to experience these things. They are practical, spiritual, often emotional and very challenging. For me the most difficult experience at that point was in dealing with rejection. I suppose what made it harder was not having a home of our own for a year. On the surface, I may have appeared strong but underneath, I felt vulnerable and very sensitive. I had unrealistic expectations of some people which did not help. Instead of looking to God, my faithful heavenly Father, I was at times looking to people as the ones to turn to. Consequently, when it did not work out quite how I had expected, I suffered disappointment. There were so many adjustments to make. If we had been cosseted in a perfect, idyllic situation, we would never have had to make these strides. I suppose it is a bit like a child learning to walk. They need to experience the knocks and to keep getting up to try again before achieving their goal.

In amongst the trials there were many blessings. The pastor of the church ran some teaching sessions on church history and Christian foundations. These were very helpful because we had the opportunity to ask questions. Learning from books and audio tapes does not afford the same benefits. My eyes were opened to the many revivals that had happened in many nations and how Christian men and women had influenced the course of history.

A trip to Chard

The Chard Christian fellowship under the watchful eye of the pastor, affectionately known as 'Uncle Sid,' had encouraged the development of some well know Christian leaders e.g., Ian Andrews and Harry Greenwood. Perhaps not so well known was a lovely lady, Joy. This lady had done some remarkable work in inner healing and deliverance. I really wanted to have the opportunity to learn from her. This is rather out of character for me, but I wrote to her, to ask for some of her valuable time. Wonderfully she responded and we set dates when I might spend a few days with her.

I borrowed a car from friends in the church, left Barrie holding the fort back home and set off in this mini clubman traveller. The car did not have a tape player so I began to sing at top voice knowing that no one else could hear me or so I thought. After a while I stopped singing only to find that it continued. What is that I thought? It was so melodious. I sang again and stopped to listen and there it was again. The light dawned. I had Angels travelling with me. I did not see anyone but perhaps whilst driving it was better that way. The singing angels accompanied me all the way to Somerset.

Joy welcomed me and shared so much. She gave me some books to look at so I spent a lot of time reading and making notes. It was an all-round eye opener. She was due to pray for a young man one afternoon and asked me if I would like to sit in with his consent? I watched what I can only describe as liquid love being poured out over him. The healing and release that followed was very moving. I had never seen ministry quite like this. The foundation of the Love of God was more powerful than anything I had witnessed in a counselling situation. And I knew that it was the reason that I had made the journey. I don't understand why I had to go to Somerset to witness this, but I am grateful anyway for the experience.

I was invited to go with Joy to visit Uncle Sid. Having heard so much about him and his wife I had a picture of them in my mind. They were nothing like I had imagined. She was working in her cottage garden in her gardening clothes and just shouted hello and waved as we went in. Uncle Sid greeted us at the door and after the introduction, he threw his arms around me and hugged me.

'You need loving' he said.

I almost cried. Joy said that I had come to learn, not for ministry but at that point I could have gone with either. I was so pleased I had met this decerning man and had the opportunity to spend time with Joy.

Another one of our most treasured experiences was 'Workshop'. This was a part time bible school for those who could not do the course full-time because of other commitments. It ran at weekends in Birmingham, all day Saturdays and Sundays. This school was run by Noel Moules. He is a Mennonite Christian and an excellent teacher (Mennonites have been called into many war zones as mediators because of their skill, courage, decerning and lack of prejudice). The course drew Christians from many denominations, cultures, and nationalities. It was so rich and embraced different forms of worship and points of views. Noel having presented multifaceted and sometimes controversial subjects, would leave us to pray and make our own decisions on where we stood. We were not spoon fed. The many different speakers from all walks of life, represented the great variety of believers belonging to a God of infinite variety. All were honoured and accepted without judgement. It was not just head learning but also a relational experience. It was not uncommon to see someone wearing leathers sitting next to a man in a suit and tie, and someone with short back and sides, talking to a person with a cockatoo haircut.

Barrie completed the course in 1992 and I completed it in 1993. We both felt really privileged to have undergone this training and experience.

The church was growing and the small building we met in was more the size of a scout hut. It was obvious that we would soon run out of space. A decision was reached that the two pastors would each run a church of their own, whilst keeping in close touch with each other. We were all asked to pray and ask God where we should worship. Two very different churches were born.

In this newly formed church, we were a part of, Barrie started to speak on a Sunday, and I got busy doing pastoral work. One day I called to see an older lady who had been really kind to our girls. She had a knitting machine and had made them all jumpers in their school colours. Esther was not yet at school but had a jumper just the same. One day when I called, the lady was really upset. Through her tears she told me that her dog had just died. She was feeling very guilty about being so upset, because after all she thought, it was only a dog! As we talked it came to light that she had lost three other close members of her family in the last couple of years. She had just carried on for the sake of the others and got on with life allowing herself no time to grieve. This dear little dog's death had opened the flood gates on all that unexpressed grief. When she realised what was happening, she was filled with relief and the guilt vanished. God was so good, and I was learning more about the miracles of inner healing.

14

Crossline

We had been settled in 'Four Winds,' for some time, when I had a dream. In this dream I was sitting on the steps of a large building looking down a road to my left. It looked like some large estate with lawns either side of the road. Coming out of the distance towards me, I could see a long trail of hundreds of people. They resembled, what I imagined wounded soldiers returning from war would look like. The only difference was they were male and female, both young and old. Some had bandages round their heads, some make-shift slings around their arms. Some had sticks to help them walk as they moved slowly along and looked as if they were in pain. I can remember saying, 'Oh God, who are these people and what can be done?' In my dream I was weeping when the reply came, 'You do something'. This dream troubled me as I had no idea who these people were or what God wanted me to do.

I had realized since our time in Wellow and involvement in the summer camps; that I needed to learn more about counselling. The Lord at that point had asked me just to reach out in love. He said that He would do the rest, but now it seemed like He was asking for something more.

The people in my dream needed more than a listening ear. Barrie had done some counsellor training as part of his youth and community course. The only experience I had had was learning on the job and reading books. I often felt unprepared, as if I had been thrown in the deep end. I felt the desire was growing in me for more input, to learn more to help those in need. We had already met so many in that place. I think that is sometimes how God works in us. He brings about a growing desire, and a dissatisfaction with the status quo to propel us forward.

Looking back, I cannot remember how the contact with 'Crossline' came about. This organisation was started in Plymouth and began as a 24/7 Christian telephone helpline. It reached out to people, many who would not set foot in a church. It seemed like the telephone was a good, partially anonymous, none threatening medium. The skills required were, a telephone, a love for people, availability, basic listening skills and a list of resources for referrals when and if required. So, the next questions were who will be listeners and who's going to train these people? It became obvious that we would need financial support as well as manpower from the church family. So, an appointment was made to speak with the two Pastors.

I was very nervous. What if they do not believe my dream or the interpretation? What if they don't think we are spiritual enough? What if they say no? These sorts of thoughts can cripple you. If the Devil was looking for a way to stop God's plans and purposes and disable His people, this is one effective way of doing it. Well, it did not happen. The pastors were very supportive, and the Help Line was given the go ahead. It was advertised in the church and the people volunteered. The founder of Crossline Plymouth came and stayed with us whilst he led the training course and then we went 'online' so-as to speak.

What started as a telephone help line, developed quickly into a face-to-face counselling service with further training. A Baptist church in the centre of the town offered us an office to begin our face-to-face work. It had a separate entrance and toilet facilities. The only payment they required was for the electricity we used. Praise the Lord. The local churches advertised the service for us and made referrals. A local organisation offered to do our call diversion service as they had someone available 24/7 on their premises. God had supplied all our needs.

The ACC (Association of Christian Counsellors) was being formed at this time and started training and accrediting counsellors. It seemed right to join with this organisation. Although I had written a basic training course to suit the work we were doing, it was not enough to take people further who wanted a more advanced professional qualification. We also linked up with another local organisation who were running a

Christian Healing retreat. Together we ran, what was then termed as, an Advanced Counselling Course. This course was written by the 'Light House' in Coventry but had been accredited by the ACC. People booked in on this two-year course and both students and trainers were monitored and supported all the way through. We had only two who did not qualify as they were not able to complete the full course.

I qualified as an advanced counsellor and trainer, but it became obvious that supervisors were needed. BAC (British Association of Counsellors) accredited supervision was very expensive and not readily available at that time, so I trained as a supervisor up to level 4.

This work stretched across thirteen years. During this time many people came to our office and accessed the telephone line. I have lost count of how many people trained in listening or counselling skills. All these people were then able to serve their church families or communities, either in a voluntary or professional capacity.

There are so many occasions that stand out, but I must tell you about a lady who came to the office. I offered her a drink and we sat down to talk. I knew nothing about her except her name. She told me she was a Jewess with so many questions about the Messiah. She started talking and for about an hour she had a conversation with God. I could only listen to her side of it and pray silently. God led this lady to Himself right in front of me, without my having to say anything apart from would you like a tea or a coffee? It was the most moving situation and at the end she hugged me and could not stop thanking me for what I had done! To an onlooker (and even to myself) I had done so very little, but God had done so much. Had we not set up Crossline, this lady would not have ended up in the office. God would not have had this opportunity to introduce her to himself, and I would not have had the privilege of witnessing this miracle. It was the perfect reminder that it is all about Him.

15

Two Lovely Young Men

We had met a vicar and his wife, from the Ludlow area, through our counselling work. Their son and his friend had enrolled to do an art foundation course at the Shrewsbury Technical College, prior to going to University. They had left it too late to get student accommodation so he phoned to ask if we knew of anyone who could help. We replied that we had a small bedroom and if necessary, we could put bunkbeds in it. They would be a bit cramped but if all else fails, they were welcome to that. Well two rather tall young men arrived with luggage, easels, and kit to squeeze into our little room. The girls loved this. It was like having two older brothers to tease and play with. The boys also seemed to enjoy the fun and gave as good as they got.

On one occasion whilst I was cleaning up stairs, I pushed the vacuum into the boys' room to find a dozen or more empty bottles of Newcastle Brown under the bunk beds. I was rather concerned that they were secretly drinking heavily and that was not a safe situation. After having a word with Barrie, he took them aside. He shared with them that we took a dim view of this and whilst they were with us, we expected that this would not happen again. They humbly agreed and no more was said. We have more recently found out that it was not the boys at all. The girls passed a pub on the way home from school and in the yard, there was a small mountain of empty beer bottles in crates. The girls decided to set the boys up and put them in an embarrassing situation. So, they had taken as many bottles as they could carry and deposited them under the boys' beds. The little monkeys had let the boys take the wrap and said nothing. I take my hat off to the boys who behaved admirably, like older brothers protecting younger sisters.

The boys had obviously enjoyed their time with us despite the hassle and came back to visit on occasions during and after their time at university. I am glad to say they both attained their degrees.

16

Romania

There have been only a few occasions in our lives that we have gone any distance without the children. Normally where one goes the others come along too. On this occasion we were invited to join a team going to Romania 1996 to help set up a counselling service in Cluj. Nicolae Ceausescu was deposed and executed at the end of 1989, so the country was still in a very poor way; the roads were full of potholes; there was very little in the shops and people had very little money to buy what was there. Most people were living in depressing flats, like giant blocks of concrete. Many did not have a kitchen and were having to cook in all weathers, on their balconies. Families had been separated and sent to locations miles apart – others killed. People did not know where their loved ones where, or even if they were alive. Society had been fragmented.

The invitation came through the couple who ran the Christian retreat. I remember the conversation I had afterwards with the Lord. It was in our garden between the rows of raspberry canes. I told Him that I didn't really have a heart for Romania. I did not know much about it (at that time) and that it had not been a country that I had thought about. Did He really want Barrie and I to go all that way? I felt Him say:

But you have a heart for people.

Well, I could not argue with that. Here was a city of people who needed loving and some help, so we agreed to go.

The team was made up of an educational psychologist, a midwifery tutor, the couple from the retreat plus Barrie and me. We were to do some counsellor training and some counselling. As none of us spoke Romanian, everything had to be done through translators. An American missionary who had gone out to Romania just after Ceausescu was deposed, was to be our link and guide. It was all arranged. We packed our cases to the limit with clothes we intended to leave there, plus the resources we needed to do the work.

We asked family and friends to look after our girls who got busy planning things to do whilst we were away. No need for concern then?

The journey was quite eventful. We flew to Bucharest (international Airport) with Lufthansa Airways. That bit was easy. Then we had to transfer across the city to catch an internal flight with the Romanian Airline 'Tarom'. This flight would then carry us from Bucharest to Cluj. The internal airport was something else. The terminal was smallish and shabby. Some of the floor tiles where missing and those that remained were uneven. The walls had been tiled at some point but now only a few were still intact. It was a two-story building with offices upstairs. The internal balcony, around the inside of the first floor, had a balustrade which was partly missing. It looked very unsafe and scary. We registered the luggage and were surprised to see the clerk handwriting our details on brown cardboard labels and tying them onto the case handles with a little string. Eventually our flight was paged, and we walked out onto the airfield. The plane looked very old but as a passenger plane, it did have windows. We noticed the Pilot was leaning out of his cockpit window, speaking to one of the ground crew. From the exhaust ports of the engine, there was a black trail of what was probably fuel or oil. It extended the full length of the aircraft. This was not boding well. We climbed up stairs that had only one handrail, into the aircraft and felt fortunate to be given seats with a back rest. Some passengers did not have that privilege nor did all seats have seat belts! The cabin service was a glass of water and a hard boiled sweet. In our anxious state, this was poor comfort. The flight route was over the Carpathian mountain range. The plane had to circle a few times to gain the required height but even so, we seemed as if we only just made it over some of the peaks. We all found ourselves praying in earnest during the flight.

We landed at night and were directed to a luggage collection point underneath a telegraph post. Mounted on the top of this post was a 'King of the Road' headlamp providing the only source of light in the darkness. The luggage eventually arrived on a tractor trailer and sitting on the top of the luggage, was an armed guard with a submachine gun. Adrenalin immediately fuelled the thoughts swimming around in my mind. Why does he need a weapon? Fortunately, the people who were meeting us had arrived and ushered us away without any further cause for worry or excitement.

We all agreed that after this experience, we would do the homeward journey to Bucharest by train.

Our time in Cluj was very busy working from early morning to late at night. If we were not teaching – we were counselling. We were hosted by local families at meal – times and were advised to count the number of people in the family before we ate. Why? Because they would only have between them, what we left. It was so moving to see their generosity, even in poverty. We soon realised that it was not a good idea to admire anything in their homes, because they would want to give it to us as a gift. This was another learning curve.

We had a diverse team each with knowledge in our own fields, so the subjects we taught on were many and varied. We met together every day, sharing areas of concern for prayer. We were all finding that people were frightened to open-up. Living under a dictator with informants in every block of flats and infiltrated into many families, made sharing very dangerous. We could not in this situation, offer a one-to-one service with a normal level of confidentiality, as we needed translators. We engaged as carefully as we could, the help of those who recognised the importance of confidentially. The people we were training also had to keep confidences as they gained the experience they needed. The vulnerable people who came for help also needed to be able to trust those who were offering the service. These were no small steps.

I will just tell you about one lady who came. Her husband drank heavily. Many of the men drank to blot out the awful pain of their situation. When drunk, this man became violent, and the family (mum and two children) were becoming increasingly scared. He had dangled the youngest child over the balcony, threatening to drop her. He held mum at knife point in front of the children, threatening to cut her throat and throw her over the balcony. Terror gripped them and only when there was a knock on the door, did he relent and let her go. There was no bolt hole for this lady, no refuge she and the children could flee to, no social security or financing. These were the kind of situations these people were facing. The service in Cluj had a huge roll to play to bring about much needed change on so many levels e.g., to help improve people's living conditions, emotional wellbeing, and safety.

Our stay lasted just short of three weeks and during that time many expressed gratitude for what we had done. A local potter had made some little wall plaques with the date on, as reminder of our visit. Another man, whose wife was ill with cancer, made me a little pot. He asked that every time I dusted it; would I pray for them? It sits on my dressing table and I have faithfully kept my promise to this day. It seemed like the help and encouragement we brought, spurred them on. It gave them hope, in what was still a very difficult situation.

On returning home I went to do some shopping in the supermarket. When the cashier was about to give me my bill, I froze. She looked uncomfortable clearly wondering what the problem was. It had just struck me that; what I was about to pay for my weekly shop would have fed a Romanian family of six for a month. It took me quite a while to adjust back again and to process some of the distressing things I had witnessed.

17

America, A Trip of a Lifetime

Whilst we were working on the summer camps we met and became friends with a young man who qualified at Leicester University in Astrophysics. He specialised in outer atmosphere weather calculations for space shots. Not many openings for this type of employment in Leicester, you might be thinking. But when he got his doctorate, he was one of only three in the world with this qualification. He was eventually head hunted and went to America to work at Boston University with links to NASA. He met and married a beautiful young American woman. Our friend, Jeremy, really wanted us to visit them in America but it was too expensive for a family of 6. They must have really wanted us to go because they sent us the money for the flights.

They also offered to organise a tour of America anywhere we wanted to go. What an offer. In the summer of 1991, we set off on a family adventure.

Helen was 18 at the time and we thought that it would probably be the last family holiday together, as young people need to spread their wings and forge their own way in the world. We wanted it to be a special time together. Jeremy's wife Ann was a wonderful organiser.

We wanted to spend time with them and whilst in America visit friends in Los Angeles and my Uncle Bob and his wife in New York. We had three weeks in which to fit it all in.

We arrived in Boston and spent a few days seeing the sights around there. There were many highlights – like standing at the top of the John Hancock tower looking down on the city and visiting the Plymouth Plantation. This small village resembled a working museum and commemorated John Robinson and the Pilgrim Fathers. They sailed with the Mayflower from Plymouth England to New England in America in 1620. It was fun to see people dressed in the costume of the time and the demonstration of how they lived their lives.

We then took a flight to Denver Colorado. Ann's parents lived at Boulder not too far away. They had left a small minibus at the airport for us to use. This enabled us to all travel together. Even more than that; they had put a large cool box in the boot full of provisions for our trip. Jeremy drove to their log cabin in the mountains at a place named' Pine'. Talk about unprecedented favour, it was amazing. The cabin plus provisions and minibus – all free of charge!

The cabin was high in the Colorado Rockies just below the tree line, wild and surrounded by wonderful tall trees. It was really quaint complete with an outside loo. Jeremy and Ann checked the cabin out for creepy crawlies and snakes, as it had not been used for some time. A relative, however had kindly been in and made up the beds. I have never seen Jeremy so animated, jumping up and down pulverising a poisonous spider with the soul of a shoe as we entered. Inside there was the sound of humming bees; they had made their home in the roof and a long honey trail ran down the inside of the plaster. Honey had seeped through the wall and become visible in the room where we slept. What a wild place! We were warned to keep a look out for snakes, spiders, and mountain lions and to keep the toilet door shut when we visited the outside Jon. I was a bit in awe, nervous as I thought about the children and how they would cope. I need not have worried; it was just another exciting adventure to them, and they loved it. Wading through streams, climbing rock faces, and exploring nature trails, it was all seen as pure fun. Barrie and Jeremy went fishing one day but caught nothing. A couple of guys who parked their car next to theirs annoyingly caught a huge fish, but the good news was that they sold it to Barrie. Fresh fish for super that night, what a treat.

From these wilds we flew from Denver to Los Angeles. We were met with flowers at the airport by our friends Art and Thordis. This lovely couple had owned a house just outside of the city; in a flash fire they had lost their property and all their treasured memories, but God protected their lives. They just had one daughter at home, who was a nurse at a local hospital. This couple now rented an apartment as they had no heart to buy again. This apartment was luxury itself. The fragrant smell of lilies filled the rooms. The bathrooms were out of this world. Thordis laundered all our clothes and there were such a lot after spending time in the cabin. We were chauffeured all over the city – Hollywood, Boulevard walk, Skid Row, and up into the mountains. The girls posed for photographs pretending to be film stars, and really got into the mood. Universal studios and Disney world were big hits.

Every night they fell into bed and immediately fell asleep with more happy memories. I kept asking myself this question. How is it possible that a one income family of six have been able to do a trip like this? Why have these lovely people wanted to show us so much love and favour? It is truly amazing, but we have an amazing God.

Next Stop – we flew to New York and met my Uncle Bob, my mother's only brother. The Big Apple as it is named, was a bustle of activity. It was loud and fast. Uncle Bob and Launa lived in an old apartment on Manhattan. They arranged to stay with friends so we could have their place to ourselves. Uncle Bob was always a bit of a joker and he said that there was a hurricane on the way. I said in an unbelieving tone 'Oh yes and what do they call this one?' He answered, 'Bob'. I laughed and took no more notice, but he was not joking!

We had a visit to China Town complete with authentic Chinese food. We also tried Italian food. The girls' eyes were like organ stops when they saw the biggest pizzas that any of us had ever seen. We visited Wall Street, the World Trade Centre, Twin Towers, the statue of Liberty and even a quick drive through the Broncs. On our way back to Boston we decided to take one of the famous Grey Hound buses. Hurricane Bob had hit the coast the day before and the road was strewn with branches and rubbish, so the journey was rather slower than normal. We saw first-hand the power of this storm and the damage it had done.

After a couple of days with Jeremy and Ann we flew back to the UK. What a trip. I had wanted a special holiday together but in my wildest dreams, I could not have imagined what God had in store! We are so grateful to all those lovely people who made it possible.

18

The Toronto Blessing

In 1994 we were beginning to hear about a supernatural move of God in Toronto. God was pouring out His Spirit on people with remarkable effects. Some people were claiming healings, both physical and emotional. Others were experiencing a closeness to God that they had not experienced before. Also in evidence were prophetic words and other gifts of Holy Spirit e.g., speaking in other tongues, interpretation of the tongues, deliverance from fears and other hinderances connected to the demonic. News of this spread all over the world and people began to travel to this area to spend a while in this spiritual atmosphere. There were reports of people in hotels, restaurants and shops experiencing God, even those who had not previously known Him or recognised that they wanted to.

My thoughts were occupied with both a question and a request. The question was – why not in England, in Shropshire, Shrewsbury, why not here? Then the request was – please do it here with us Lord. It seemed that some who had visited Toronto and returned to their own nation, town and family had carried the anointing back with them. The more I thought about this, the more it occurred to me that we could be a part of the answer to our own prayers.

One morning whilst talking to the Lord, I really sensed that Barrie and I should book a flight and go to Toronto. This was a bit of a change for me because I had previously felt that this blessing should come to us. I rang Barrie at school which again was something I would only have done in an emergency. The secretary then had to leave her post to request that Barrie come to the phone. Another teacher had to be found to cover his class for him whilst he was away. But this seemed so important . . . worth the interruption and Barrie knew that it had to be for me to disturb him at work. He agreed, and I booked the flight and a hotel near the Airport Vineyard church, as it was titled at that time.

Because this was in term time, Barrie requested a couple of days off either side of the weekend. There was no guarantee that it would be allowed but God organised that as well – as unpaid leave. This again was a first for Barrie.

Two friends of ours happened to be going at the same time so we joined forces. We did several sight-seeing trips together, one being to the spectacular Niagara Falls. We had asked the girls what gift we could bring back for them and Helen had asked for a plain black umbrella. There was a shop near the falls that sold only umbrellas, of every colour, design, and size. I had never seen a shop like this in the UK. Needless-to-say we found a black umbrella. As the wind was carrying the spray from the falls in our direction, we decided to make use of it, perhaps just once. On unfurling this item, we were surprised to find written in strong white letters around the circumference, 'S**t it's raining!'. Now there were others we recognised from the Vineyard church also visiting the falls. This posed a bit of a dilemma. Do we keep the umbrella up and stay dry, risking the embarrassment of others seeing the rude word? Or do we take it down and get wet? We kept it up.

This church is the only church we have ever had to queue to get in. You might think that this is strange, well – so did we. As we queued however, we talked to people from all over the world and shared experiences together. The time just flew by. The meetings lasted at least 2 hours, but it seemed like only minutes. The presence of God was almost tangible. It wrapped itself around you like a warm blanket and people shared at the end of the meetings what God had done for them. There were some unusual manifestations; some people just dropped to the floor and lay there peacefully for quite a time while others who were perhaps more excited and vocal were kindly asked to go into side rooms, so as not to disturb the others. As this was new to so many, it was not easy for some to know how to navigate their way through this different encounter with God, but help was available should anyone need it.

I must just tell you about a prayer group we joined one afternoon. There were over thirty people from several nations. A Russian lady prayed in a language she did not speak or read as some Chinese visitors sitting next to us, heard about the Father God's love for them, in Mandarin. They translated what the Russian lady had spoken for her benefit and for ours. It was beautiful.

We really wanted to carry this anointing back to UK but how do you know if you are carrying enough anointing for it to be evident and effective? We did not have long to wait. Back home we prayed for some people and the effects spoke for themselves. People were struck by the power of God and some were overcome with joy; some experienced emotional and physical healings; we had more prophetic words for people regarding things that we had no way of knowing in the natural and prayers were answered in similar ways to those we had witnessed in Toronto.

We visited one of the local church leaders on our return to England, to share some research work we had done on a pastoral subject. Whilst sitting in the lounge, their phone rang in the hall. We heard him pick up the phone and say hello before falling backwards into the lounge. The joy of God overcame him, and he was unable to either get up or take his call. The phone was just left dangling. He was overcome with laughter and a joy that wiped away all the stress he had been under. Then finally he just lay there in God's presence. We also experienced the joy, but just sat motionless on his sofa for the duration. He had also visited a centre in London where they had experienced this anointing, so he had a double portion of blessing that night. We never got round to the business we had gone to discuss but God did what was most important.

19

A Wedding with a difference

Whilst we were living in Shrewsbury Helen met her beau. Paul sang and played his guitar in a well-known local rock band. This very kind and talented young man came into Helen's life at just the right time, and they fell in love. Paul arranged for us to meet his family over a meal at a local pub. He had told his parents and his brother and wife, that we were 'religious'.

We decided to have a bit of fun with this idea and Barrie made himself a dog collar by cutting up a white plastic milk bottle. He dressed in a dark suit with his dog collar and looked every inch the respectable vicar. They were all waiting when we entered the restaurant area and the looks on their faces were a cross between amazement and shock. Paul's brother whispered, not too softly to him:

Bleep, Bleep, you did not tell me he was a bleep vicar!

We did confess a bit later in the evening, when the stiff dog collar became uncomfortable, and Barrie took it off.

Helen and Paul got married at St Giles church in August 1995. That summer was particularly hot, and dry. Our grass was scorched yellow and brown. We realised that fresh flowers would not survive in this heat so, we acquired enough silk and dried flowers for the wedding bouquets and decorations.

Helen wanted me to make her wedding dress and she mostly designed it herself. With her long dark hair, she looked beautiful in a 'snow white' style dress in white satin with a dark blue taffeta laced bodice. She did not want a wedding car but wanted to walk to church with her dad. When asked, what happens if it rains? She replied that they could use an umbrella! It did not rain, the weather was beautiful. As they walked toward St Giles church, the neighbours came out to cheer them on. People waved, some tooted their car horns and all in all, it was wonderful.

Ok, so what about a reception? A Marque in the garden with sandwiches and a barrel of beer would be great, was the reply. They did not want people involved whom they did not know so we asked friends to help. We were, however, a bit stumped over where we could source a Marque. We were still mulling this over when a friend who worked for the parks department said that they had ones that they hired out. Problem solved. This marque was a bit like a small circus tent with two support poles each with guy ropes to hold them upright. One guy rope even had to be secured to our plum tree. We were told that its size was approximately that of our dried-up lawn but when it came it was bigger than we had anticipated. It covered the vegetable plot and the raspberry canes as well. What were we going to do? Barrie came up with:

If you cannot change something, make it a feature.

Out came the fairy lights. The veg and raspberry canes were transformed into a pretty lighting feature in the corner of the marque.

Another friend who was an expert cake maker set too and created a cake in the shape of a fairy castle in blue and white. It even had turrets. Another couple came and organised the bar. Other friends came and helped set up the cold buffet and others the Bar B Q. My sister and I decorated the marque with blue swags, ribbons and dried flowers. Esther did little flower arrangements over every tent peg so people would notice them and not fall over.

Our friends Art and Thordis came from Los Angeles. Uncle Bob and Aunty Lorna came from New York. Together with other family and friends we made up the wedding party.

Paul already had a semidetached house in Cross Houses which they lovingly called 'High Cross Hall'. So, Helen and Paul had somewhere of their own to start their married life.

They now have two wonderful grown-up boys, and we have two very tall and delightful grandsons.

20

Constant Change
is Here to Stay

The government were offering enhanced pensions for older members of staff that wanted to retire early from teaching. Barrie took advantage of this incentive and retired from Adams Grammar School in 1996. He wanted to do work for the church before he felt he was too old. It just seemed that everything was lining up for change.

With Helen married, Kate at University in Hull studying Law and Erica in Manchester training to become a nurse; it only left Esther aged 16, still at home. We had been helping a church in Newport with some counselling and pastoral work and began to feel that our time living in Shrewsbury was coming to an end. However, we did not want to move until Esther was in- agreement. Shrewsbury was the only home she remembered, and she had a large friendship base. In fact, when the other girls brought friends home, they came in ones and twos. Not so with Esther, she would arrive with four or five or more – consequently the orange juice and biscuits would rapidly disappear. We continued to pray and eventually Esther said that if she could continue her schooling in

Shrewsbury through to the Sixth Form College, she would be willing to move. This meant her travelling most days by bus but that did not seem to faze her. We put the house on the market and began to look round for a new home.

Just on the outskirts of Newport there was a lovely estate of new houses being built and there was one house left. It just so happened that it was the design we felt would work for us. It had a downstairs study which would serve well as a counselling room without affecting anyone else at home. It had a double garage which Barrie could use as a workshop. The garden was a good size with room for the plants we had acquired and cuttings that we had taken in preparation for a move. It had four bedrooms, so plenty of room for the girls when they came home. Another bonus, or should I say miracle, we were offered it for a reduced price as it was the last one to sell.

We started to think about a name for our new home and Esther said it must be something to do with breath. We immediately thought of the Scripture in Ezekiel which reads 'Come from the four winds oh breath and breathe on these slain that they might live'[11]. As you know our home in Shrewsbury was 'Four Winds' and we were coming from Four Winds to our new home. So, we named our new house Ruach (which is the Hebrew for breath). How had Esther known about the breath and the link regarding our house names? We just knew God was in this move.

Moving was not easy in one sense. Our eldest daughter and husband had to adjust to Mum and Dad being a bit further away. We had to tell our friends, neighbours, house group and church in Shrewsbury that we felt God was bringing about a change. We also needed to have a rethink about how we were to organise our life, our finances, and commitments. In a way, I think we were still looking like Abraham, for the city whose builder and architect was God. Looking for our place in the church that Jesus said He would build; the one that the gates of Hell would not prevail against. Something of that longing expressed in the Lord's Prayer; Thy Kingdom come, Thy, will be done on earth as it is in heaven; Something of that pilgrim spirit that is still very much alive in us from our time living at Columba Folk.

PART 3

21

New House

We moved in April 1997. Our new home had been carpeted and everywhere was clean and shiny. What a blessing not to have any major repairs urgently requiring our attention. Just the nice cosmetic things like putting up curtains, blinds and our pictures.

Prior to our move, I had had the pleasure of planning the gardens, front and back. I had allowed myself 30 mins/day to let my imagination run riot with designs. I love plants, flowers, and gardens so I really enjoyed this space for creativity. By the time we moved in I had allocated a place for every plant and shrub. Whilst most people would have been attending to the inside of a house, I was digging over the back garden. The plants were put in their places and the borders marked out. I raked and rolled the central area and laid the lawn. What a joy. What I had pictured in my mind was coming into shape.

Barrie got on with putting up the curtain tracks and measuring for the blinds. It all seemed to be done in no time, even between visits from friends and family. Many came bearing house-warming gifts and some were plants. Yippee!

We were soon back doing our pastoral and counselling work both in Newport and in Shrewsbury. It was a few years later we felt that the Lord say it was time to close Crossline down (more about this in Chapter 23). God's timing and instructions are sometimes hard to explain, and it is often after the event that the understanding comes. God wants us to move in faith; the faith that gives us the confidence that what we hoped for, will in reality happen.

Renewal meetings were still being held in the area both in Telford and Newport. We continued to witness God's miraculous hand bringing people to know Him with healings physical and emotional, deliverance (from the things that rob people of their freedom) and supernatural provision in the form of finances, goods, jobs etc . . .

22

A Romance in the air

Kate having completed her Law degree with a 2;1 with honours, returned home that summer. Not to the old house, Four Winds' but to Ruach. The girls had chosen their rooms and Kate's looked out over the front garden. It was so lovely to have her home, but we realised that she would need transport to get around. We spotted a small Fiat BIZ 125 car which was a bit whacky but served the purpose. She worked in a local hotel for a while and then trained and qualified as a financial advisor working for a local company. Afterwards she moved on and worked as a legal advisor to The National Farmers Union. Following her time at Law School, she started work as a solicitor for a local Shrewsbury firm.

By the September, after her time in Hull, Luke, a young man who she had met whilst doing her degree, was desperate to see her again. He had returned home to Kent after getting his degree but was really missing her. Kate asked if he could come and stay for a week. *Lovely* we thought and he can use Erica's room as she was still in Manchester. The week turned into two weeks and then it became obvious that there was no way he was going home. He got himself a job at a factory to pay his way and by the November he had met with Jesus. We were at a Christian meeting in London when Holy Spirit touched Luke. Such was the power of the encounter he could hardly stand and needed support to get back to his seat. I did not tell him at the time, but everything he touched had been prayed over including his laundry and a 'Jar Jar Binks' soft toy from the Star Wars saga. This toy was the source of much fun and games. We would find him in cupboards, balanced over doors so he fell on you when you entered, seated on the lights, and wrapped in towels in the bathroom. We would sometimes hide it and Luke would play hide and seek to find Jar Jar. Eventually, in a very grubby state, he ended up in the washing machine, Jar Jar, not Luke!

His Mum and Stepdad came up for a weekend to stay with us. We all got on so well together and we began to pray for them also. That took rather longer but after 17 years they are now firmly in the Kingdom of God and loving it.

Luke proposed to Kate on Christmas day 1997 and they got married the following May. They had negotiated the purchase of a small cottage in Newport. The church family organised an amazing reception for 250 guests. Not sure how they did it, but it ran like clockwork. Kate and Luke then moved into their new home to start their lives together.

Luke had not known what to do with his degree but was beginning to look towards teaching. He went back to college and qualified as a history teacher. They both really wanted children, but nothing seemed to happen on that front. Helen had Dudley and Wesley, Erica had Joseph and Kate was desperate. She had visited an infertility clinic and found out that she had a condition that would make it impossible to conceive naturally. They tried IVF without being offered much hope of success. In the meantime, Luke had had a Scripture and prophetic word that their sons would sit around their table. My mother had a prophetic word about a year before she died, that Kate would have babies on her knee in around a year's time. Here we have the tension between faith in God's word verses the medical prognosis. God won and they miraculously had twins followed by two more sons. They all have healthy appetites and sit regularly around their table. How faithful our God is?

Both Kate and Luke have had other career moves but continue to trust God for themselves and their lovely Family.

Counselling; Advanced Training Course

In 1997, Along with the couple from the Christian retreat, we realised that we needed to provide ongoing training for those who had done the basic counselling course. There was nothing being offered in the area with a Christian foundation.

An organisation in Coventry called 'The lighthouse' had developed an advanced counselling course accredited by the Association of Christian Counsellors (ACC). As we were already working and associated with the ACC, the Light House course seemed like a good choice. We asked if they would franchise the course out to us, to run it locally? They agreed. We advertised and started the training in the September. It ran over two years, training about 30 students and all but 2 qualified.

The Christian retreat was closed about a year after the completion of advanced course. The couple who had run it were struggling with ill health and needed a quieter life. They had given so much, and it was time to have a rest.

23

Second Trip to Romania 1998

It had been a couple of years since our last trip to Romania when we were approached again with an invitation to return. We were asked to continue some of the work we had had the privilege of starting. The Romanians had asked specifically for Barrie and me, to go.

We had been doing some work with adult survivors of childhood sexual abuse, so along with a lot of other teaching material we packed our cases full to the brim. We were not sure just exactly what they had planned, so we wanted to be prepared. When we arrived at the railway station in Cluj, there was no one to meet us. We thought this was a little strange and waited for a while before taking a taxi to our accommodation. Once there we contacted the American missionary to ask what she had organised. It transpired that there had been some relationship difficulties and we were needed, amongst other things, to mediate and pour oil on some troubled waters.

The next big surprise came in the form of a weekend conference. It had been organised for the middle weekend of our stay. The press, church ministers, local doctors, medics, the city mayor with dignitaries, and everyone who was (considered to be) a someone, had been invited. The blow came when we were told, YOU are the speakers, and your subject is sexual abuse! Gosh we thought; We would have our work cut out for us!

The conference began on the Friday evening and ran through to and included the Saturday evening. Somehow, we had to cover the many facets of this large subject over those 27 hours. One area we had no idea we would need to address surfaced on the Friday night. Amongst these people, many believed that if a child was sexually abused it was the child's fault. A common belief was that attention seeking children were promiscuous and thereby encouraging abuse. We realised that we needed to put some Biblical principals in place, regarding adult responsibility. It seemed like a rocky start but so important to address this issue.

The Saturday ran much more to plan and many commented that it had been valuable to visit this subject alongside of a biblical perspective. The press reports were also favourable. We were glad to have a rest on the Sunday and spent the day with a local Pastor and his family. They asked us if we would consider moving to Cluj and learning the language so we could continue to help them. It was heart-warming to be asked but we both knew that our place was back home.

The rest of our visit, for the most part was similar – to our first, counsellor training and counselling appointments. We did however do a little mediation to address the relational difficulties and misunderstandings that had occurred. When we left, we felt that things were in a better place. The community also, in those two years had moved on. There was more in the shops, more people smiling and a growing sense of freedom and hope. Thankfully things were changing for the better.

After this second Romanian trip, the Lord began to speak to us about closing Crossline down. This was a difficult decision for me as I was torn between conflicting thoughts. Was I letting God down? After all He had given me the dream that led to its formation. After 13 years, was it time to do something different? To make it more difficult some of the local clergy were asking:

Where will we send our people who need help?

It was quite a struggle.

Eventually the Lord showed me that as we had trained hundreds of people to a basic level and had trained others at a more advanced level, that these people were now placed and ready to take on the work in their own localities. With this in mind, we were able to bring the Crossline service to a close. It is often the case that as one door closes others open, and over the years many with needs have somehow found themselves at our door, requiring a listening ear and counselling.

24

Ever Heard of Twitterpated?

Years ago, we watched Walt Disney's Bambi. In this film during springtime, the birds and other animals were falling in love. It was called being twitterpated. This word seems to have stuck and every time we notice someone falling for someone, we look at each other and say knowingly 'TWITTERPATED?'

As a child, Erica would bring home stray cats and dogs, even if they were not really lost. She had the habit of gathering up any who seemed to need a bit of love and attention. It was really no surprise that she chose a career in nursing, it really suited her down to the ground.

Erica qualified as a nurse in 1999 and guess what? She returned home bringing her fiancée back with her. They were well and truly TWITTERPATED. You might be forgiven for thinking this is becoming a familiar story. When the girls went off to university, we never expected that they would gravitate home. Our expectation was that they would be in different parts of the world doing their own thing, only returning home for short visits.

Erica's beau, Craig, had been full time in the army and he asked me one day:

Is there room in God's church for a squaddie?

It touched my heart and I told him:

Yes, there is room for you, you can be a soldier in the Lord's army.

This lovely young man now works for an engineering company that repairs army equipment known as small arms. He is studying part time for a degree in engineering and doing well. After years of believing that he was not academic and would achieve nothing; he is finding out that God has placed some wonderful gifts and skills into his life. He is also a great dad to two wonderful young people, and we are so proud of him and what he has achieved.

Erica had struggled with her studies; we found out when she was in secondary education that she was dyslexic but did not realise how much it was affecting her reading and writing. However, this did not stop her because her determination was greater than any handicap. She is now in charge of diabetic care across two hospitals and lectures nationally in her subject. Her story is a real encouragement to those who are experiencing similar struggles. Whilst I am writing this, I am feeling overwhelmed by what she has achieved.

Erica and Craig got married in 2000. I think mum making the wedding dresses had become a bit of a tradition. I had the joy and the challenge of making Helen's and Kate's and now true to form, Erica turned up with a pattern. We chose the fabric during a trip to

Birmingham. It was great to work on her dress together, and those of her bridesmaids.

A couple of years later, when they were nicely settled into their own home, Joseph was born. What a sweety. Barrie looked after him for three years before he went to nursery and as a result, Jo is very close to his Granddad.

25

Not as Planned

In 2001 we realised that we did not feel at home in the church we were attending. Our work there was done so we quietly withdrew. We did not want to cause a fuss or division. Some people approached us afterwards asking if we were going to set up a church or have meetings? We were not in the place where we wanted to do either but said that we were going to have a night of worship and prayer once a week. We told them that they would be welcome to join us if they wanted, but that it was only a gathering of friends not a church. Very soon there were quite a few people filling our lounge. We would worship for an hour or more, giving back to God the only things we could give Him, our love, worship, and praise. Sometimes His presence was so strong that we had to sit in silence for around half an hour, not able or wanting to move. We asked the people who came, to only come if they really wanted to, but to other wise please stay away. The atmosphere was so wonderful. We knew that if people came for the wrong reasons, it would spoil it. They understood. People were free to come and to go, no strings. A lot of the things that we had previously viewed as important relating to church, were no longer of any significance. Our focus was on loving God and each other.

The love and support that grew between this group of people has forged lasting friendships.

26

Angelic Encounters
2002

For some time, I had been praying to see angels. I had experienced angels singing whilst I was driving to Chard. But I believed, following two years prayer, we were about to experience some amazing encounters.

I had always wanted to visit the flower auctions in Holland at Aalsmeer and this particular year it was the big celebration of Floriade. It only happens once every ten years, so it was a wonderful opportunity to see both. Together with two close friends we had decided to do a Spring tour beginning in Holland, moving through Germany, Denmark on our way to Norway. Barrie had been to Norway when he was a young man with a youth group, but our friends and me had never seen it.

In Holland we stayed at the picturesque 'Kaag', which was a little island linked to the mainland by a small ferry. From here we visited the flower markets, the Keukenhof Gardens, and the wonderful exhibitions of the Floriade. The Dutch are so creative and have led the world in flower art for many years. It was like paradise to a gardener or florist.

Our plan was to have bed and breakfast in a hotel and an evening meal in a restaurant. For lunch we intended to buy provisions to make sandwiches to eat with a little fruit. We allowed ourselves a daily budget of what we could spend and for the most part stuck to it. One day we had done some sight-seeing and were looking for a supermarket to buy our lunch. We could not find one anywhere. We were standing on a street of small terrace houses, about to pray. When next to us, from inside one of these houses stepped a very tall young man carrying a shopping bag. He looked too big to be living there but in excellent English he said:

Can I help you?

We told him that we were looking for a supermarket and could not find one. He just said:

Follow me.

He was tall with long legs and we had trouble keeping up with him. Eventually we came out in a square with car parking and at the end was a large building with steps leading up to it. This was the supermarket on the ground floor with flats above it. He walked in just ahead of us. We wanted to thank him, but he was nowhere to be seen. With his height he would have been visible towering above the shelves. We separated and walked up and down the isles thinking perhaps he had bent down to pick something up, but no! Where was he? That was strange. Not having found him, we did our shopping and left.

We had planned a route through Germany for the next leg of the journey and ear-marked a hotel in the travel books we had taken with us. We found the little village where the hotel was located, a mile or so off the Autobahn. We parked the car behind the hotel and walked round to the front to find the entrance. When we found it, we knocked on the door? We could hear people inside and see that the lights were on but could not get anyone's attention. We looked again around the back but still the same story. Back on the empty street we were debating what to do next when an older couple stood next to us and asked in perfect English:

Can we help you?

We explained that we wanted to stay at this hotel, and they said:

You don't want to stay here; go back the way you came and take the first right – the hotel on the left-hand corner is clean and reasonable. You will be comfortable there.

We turned to each other and I asked:

Shall we do that?

The others nodded in assent and we turned to thank the couple, but they were nowhere to be seen. That was rather strange, we thought and how did they know which way we had come? Our car was not visible from this street and there were several ways into this village? We also noticed that they looked shinny clean and, in that way, not unlike the tall man in Holland.

Well, we did as they suggested and went back the way we had come and finding the Hotel just as they had said, we booked in. That night I had a dream. In my dream we were standing at a hotel reception asking the price of a double room and if two rooms were available? The receptionist consulted her screen and replied;

£100 per room.

Oh, that is more than we can afford. I stated with a little disappointment.

The receptionist then asked: how much can you afford?

We have a budget of £60/day: I said.

She consulted her screen again, turned and smiled:

You can have the rooms for £60.

I thought it was rather an odd dream but the following day we were to witness another miracle.

Having moved through Germany we were now in Denmark. A short look round Copenhagen and we were back on the road. We had not booked anywhere to stay, so we stopped at a Hotel we had spotted at the side of the road. At the reception we found that they had two double rooms but the price was too high and to my surprise the conversation followed as it had in my dream. We were given the rooms for the price we could afford. Hallelujah. The rooms were more like apartments with a kitchen, sitting room and bedroom with en suite. We felt really well looked after.

The following day we set off for Norway. We caught the ferry across to Kristiansand full of excitement, and began to look for accommodation. At the first Hotel we went to, the manager came out and told us that there was a nationwide strike of hotel workers! He said that although many were closed, there were a small number of Hotels it did not apply to. Consequently, due to the increased demand and reduced capacity; they were being booked up very quickly:

You could try the Rica hotel that is not far away, he continued.

We really did not have a choice so we went in search of it. Fortunately, they did have two double rooms so we immediately took them. Our friends' room however had not been cleaned after the last guest. Back down at the reception they were given the bridle suit for the same price plus an apology. It was a beautiful room and we all breathed a sigh of relief.

The next morning when Barrie and our friend went to check out, the Hotel manager was at the reception.

Barrie tells the next part of the story.

As the manager was processing our bill, we engaged in easy conversation. He asked where we were going next? We told him we had planned to drive to Voss but we needed somewhere to stay on route; perhaps Odda. He asked if we had booked ahead:

No, I replied.

He kindly offered to ring some Hotels to make the bookings for us, as not everywhere was open. He contacted Hotels in Odda only to find that they were either closed or fully booked. He then said that Rica had a hotel not far away in Morgedal, in the Telemark area, would that do? Realising the difficulties, we were happy to go with his suggestions:

What is your intended route, he asked?

I replied that we wanted to visit Voss and then make our way to Bergen in order to catch the ferry home. He rang round hotels in Voss and they were also fully booked or closed but suggested that Rica had a hotel at Ulvik and one in Bergen. He rang them and made the bookings. Although we did not speak much Norwegian, we could tell by the tone of his voice and the occasional word, that he was saying he wanted something special for his English visitors. Having made all the bookings for the required number of days.

He then asked me: How old are you?

I raised my eyebrows and replied: Is that something you should be asking a friend?

He laughed and went on to explain that Rica hotels had a senior's program. Those over 65 that book three nights in a Rica Hotel get the fourth night free of charge.

I replied: I am over 65 but the other three in our party are not.

He stamped four senior members cards and said: They will not ask!

Our journey took us through some wonderful scenery and quite an adventure at a road side convenience. My friend Isabell, had never come across a toilet that was a squatter. She looked at it and could not decide the best way to use it; forward or backward, stand or bend down? Out of sheer desperation she tackled it like a true Brit. After much laughing and comments of exasperation she managed to move on.

We arrived at this huge impressive Hotel at Morgadal. It was obvious by the empty car park that they did not have many guests. At reception we were told that they were between seasons; the winter skiing and summer walking and water sport holidays. We had not known that the famous Telemark skiing was invented here. Having put our luggage in our rooms we went for a swim before dinner. Despite the fact we were the only people in there, a tray with hot coffee and four cups had been left at the side of the pool. How did they know we would go for a swim?

At dinner the waitress came to take our order. She announced that because of the lack of visitors, the chef was bored:

Order what you like and he will make it for you, she said.

We were amazed, nothing like that had ever happened to us. After the wonderful meal we were asked if we would like to sit in the lounge for coffee? When we were comfortably settled, the waitress arrived with not only the coffee but beautifully wrapped gifts for Isabell and myself. Inside were wonderfully illustrated books about the history of the area and Telemark skiing. Wow, what a surprise and what a joy.

The following day we drove to Ulvik where we had booked four nights at the Rica Brakanes hotel. The hotel was again magnificent. It was situated at the end of a fiord with magnificent views. Having booked in, we went to find our rooms on the first floor. All the carpets were royal blue and very striking, but when we got to our corridor, we had red carpets. Oh, we felt like VIPs. On entering our amazing rooms, each with a balcony, we could see down the length of this fabulous fiord. It took our breath away.

At dinner that night the waiter told us that they were expecting a tour of people to arrive the following evening so, if we wanted, we could come half an hour earlier to avoid any delays. We wondered if this was normal practice or if we were being singled out for special treatment? Either way it felt good.

We had wanted to do a tour called, 'Norway in a Nutshell'. It embraced a trip by boat, road, miniature gage railway and modern train journey. Barrie had done this one-day trip many years ago and we really wanted to experience it. Needless to say, it did not disappoint us.

We had also picked up the details of two walks, with an English translation, from the hotel reception. The first one was supposed to be about three hours but we got a bit stuck. We had walked along this long straight narrow lane leading from a road up the side of a hill. Every couple of hundred yards there were clues but we had lost the trail. The directions said to look for a gravel path to our left but we could not find it. On the lane once again, we were debating what to do. When standing next to us was a young man who asked in perfect English if he could help us. He took us by surprise as, even with a clear view down the lane, we had not seen him approach. We explained that we were looking for a gravel path and that we could not find it. We even showed him our directions. He looked at them and commented that the directions were certainly was not very clear but he encouraged us to keep looking for the clues. Then he set off up the hill, as he was going to meet up with some friends. We decided that we would carry on a little further up the hill to look for this path. We had walked quite a way and no gravel path was to be found anywhere, when the young man returned back down the hill to us. He announced that he did not think that we were going in the right direction and it would be better if we turned back. He then turned around and retraced his steps. This was all becoming rather strange. We carried on and came to a stream. Feeling hungry we had stopped there for our lunch when the young man came back yet again. He repeated that the way ahead was definitely the wrong path for us and that we should turn around and go back. We offered to share our lunch with him but he politely declined. He said, glancing over his shoulder, that he needed to go as he was going to be late. At that point we decided to retrace our steps and as we passed a grassy path (which was now on our right), we noticed some clues a little way up that we had not seen beforehand. By now we had realised the directions were not entirely accurate. We realised that the gravel path was indeed the grassy path and completed our walk safely. How odd. This rather shiny young man did not leave us until he was sure we would turn back. After that we did not see him again.

The confusing instructions of the first walk did not put us off. We considered doing the second walk, but wanted to check out the details before we set off. We walked into town to the visitors' centre but unfortunately it was closed; everything was closed and the street was empty. It took a moment or two to realise it was a Sunday. Of-course it is quiet.

We were just discussing what to do, when this very unusual looking man stood beside us and asked in perfect English:

Can I help You?

He looked so bright and his eyes were so vivid but warm. His beard was plaited and reached down his chest to an ornate clasp. I thought he resembled an Aztec God. We explained what we wanted to do and the difficulties we had had during the previous walk. He looked at the instructions and the map and commented:

You would think that intelligent people could produce something better than this wouldn't you?

He pointed up the hill to a barn painted red and gave us instructions from there. We turned to each other to confer. Shall we chance it? We turned back to say thank you and he was gone.

The street was empty when he appeared so where did he come from? The street was empty when he disappeared so where did he go? If we had missed the clues from our previous encounters, this was so blatantly obvious we could not miss it.

What do angels look like? Well, the ones we met were very different but they all had shiny faces, and they all helped us with directions along the way[10]. They each spoke in perfect English. They appeared and disappeared in supernatural ways. They had supernatural knowledge and insights. We were very grateful for their interventions and thanked God for them even before we realised who they were.

Our holiday finished as beautifully as it started and we will never forget it.

27

A Surprise Turn or Two

After running Crossline and spending much time counselling, training and supervising, I really felt that I wanted a change. Esther had passed her A levels and was now at University in Northampton studying Politics with Sociology. So, all of a sudden, I had some time on my hands. I had mentioned to the family that I would like a little job working with plants or flowers. Something more resembling a hobby, just for pleasure.

We had arrived back from a short holiday in Ibiza, to be met at the airport by Luke. On the way home he announced:

By the way, I have got you a job!

What do you mean? I replied shocked.

He went on to tell us that he had been walking down Newport High Street when he noticed a poster in the window of the florist. It was advertising for an assistant. He had gone in and spoken to the manager to ask if the vacancy had been filled as the job would suit his mother-in-law down to the ground. He told her that we were on holiday but we would be back by the weekend and that I had had lots of experience (Really don't know where he got that from). The vacancy had not been filled, so he arranged an interview for me the following Tuesday. Some things you just could not make up. I decided although it all seemed so whacky, that it could be exactly what I had been looking for.

I turned up for the interview on the Tuesday. It was all very informal. The manager after the usual introductions showed me the Inter flora book of designs and asked me to do one of them. I don't think I did it very well but then the shop got really busy. The manager was holding the 'fort' on her own so I rolled up my sleeves and worked until the rush subsided. I was paid for the afternoons work and given the job. This was heaven, like being paid for playing. I loved it. Buckets and buckets of wonderful flowers and foliage.

The other members of staff were lovely. They helped me get to know the ropes and we had so much fun whilst getting on with the job. I enjoyed the experience so much that I enrolled at Reese Heath College at Nantwich for a two-year course in floristry, finishing with a distinction in all subjects. I think it was the most expensive gift I have given myself – the course was expensive but so enjoyable. I still love being creative with flowers; planning events like weddings and other functions when the opportunity presents itself.

I had been working at the florists for some time when the government began recruiting for radiographers to return to practice. There was a national shortage of allied health professionals. As I was only working part time,

I began to think that perhaps I could help. I applied and did a short retraining program and started work at the local hospital. God works in mysterious ways. I think I must have been the only Radiographer in the department who had never had an interview. It all just seemed to fall into place. My work at the florist drew to a close as my work at both the Princess Royal Hospital and the Cottage Hospital in Newport took more of my time. What great opportunities had opened up that reconnected me with another job I loved. I joined the professional body, The Society of Radiographers, and did some work for their 'Return to Practice' group. I even managed to get a paper published in the professional journal which stimulated interest in several countries.

One day whilst working in the CT department, one of the Radiologists asked me:

You are religious aren't you, Georgina. What church do you go to?'

I had never advertised the fact that I was a Christian, but somehow, they all knew. I can remember saying that I did not really like the word religious as it had many unpalatable associations (with war, hypocrisy etc) but if they asked me if I loved Jesus, then the answer is Yes. The rest of the conversation had to wait for another time as patients needed our attention.

28

The End of Mums Earthly Journey

Mum and Dad moved to Shrewsbury from Hull to be close to the family. Mum had been diagnosed as having pancreatic cancer and dad had realised that he needed help with caring for mum. Heather had managed to get a pensioner's bungalow for them. Despite the shortage of this type of accommodation one just so happened to be available at the right time. Mum and dad celebrated their diamond wedding anniversary after their move to Shropshire, with all their growing family around them. We gave thanks for their many years together.

Mum had requested to die at home and with nursing help and night sitters we were able to arrange it. Each morning one of us would be there to relieve the night sitter so mum and dad were not left on their own.

This particular day in 2005, Kate and Luke had just relieved the nurse who was the night sitter. After taking off their coats they entered the bedroom and said hello to mum and dad. After hearing their familiar voices, mum died peacefully knowing Dad had the support he needed at hand. Kate had asked me three days before, what she should do if mum died whilst she was with her and I was able to run through what would be required. So, even our sad memories are accompanied by the knowledge of God's love and faithful provision.

One of the GP practice nurses told us that one day whilst she was with her, Mum was having a conversation with the Lord. She told Jesus that she was coming. The nurse was touched and knew the time was near. She added that Mum's faith had helped her make the transition.

29

Another Romance

Esther returned home in 2002 after attaining her degree and got a job working for a local company doing admin, whilst applying to work for an IT company in Birmingham as a team leader in charge of various projects. It was whilst working there that she met her now husband, a lovely man named Devdeep. His family originated from the Punjab India, but Dev was born in London. They became an item, well and truly 'Twitterpated'.

Because we are a white Christian family and Dev's family are Sikhs originally from India, Esther and Dev were both very sensitive about how they broached the news. The Sikh tradition incorporates arranged marriages, so Dev was breaking with tradition in more than one way. Dev's Mum and Dad are lovely people and as we got to know more about each other, we have become really good friends. We are able to talk about our beliefs along with many other subjects and enjoy each other's company. Love builds bridges.

Babbo Gets Married

You have probably had pet names for people as we have. When she was little, Esther had called me Mammo and Barrie Daddo. We named her Babbo because she is our youngest.

In 2007 Babbo married Dev. You will possibly have guessed that it was a wedding with an Indian flavour. In fact, she was by appearances married three times over. Let me explain. Esther wanted a Christian service but Sikh families (hope I have understood this correctly) do not recognise a marriage unless the couple have walked round their holy book three times.

After much prayer and wanting to honour our new family, we organised a large marque in the grounds of Longford Hall; a boarding facility for Adams Grammar school (where Barrie had worked for many years). It was a beautiful setting for the marriage service which Barrie had the privilege and joy of conducting. Then all the guests were invited to the Gurdwara at Wednesfield for the (Anand Karaj Gurudwara) Sikh service. Here there was also a registrar present, in a separate office, who conducted the legal side of things.

Three services in one day and then the reception again at Longford Hall. Around 360 guests were catered for amongst whom was our newest addition to the family, our very first granddaughter Iona. We had the most amazing Indian food, plus a chocolate fountain that went down really well with the kids big and small. It was a special day and we were especially touched by Dev's dad's speech. It was obviously a difficult time for them, blending their traditional practices with ours and knowing that members of their family had also struggled. He bravely talked about arranged marriages and said that they had arranged the catering, Barrie and I had arranged the venue, flowers etc and Dev had arranged to meet and marry Esther. All had been arranged in the best tradition. This was a masterpiece of diplomacy. Well done Maninder (Dev's dad)

Esther and Dev were buying a small house in Newport and after a wonderful but exhausting day, they were able to retreat to their own home and relax before a break in the Lake District.

When Esther was at the Wakeman School in Shrewsbury; the school organised a student exchange with an area in Austria. Esther took part and made friends with an Austrian girl named Monica. They seemed to have a similar sense of humour and managed to get into a few scrapes together. Monica and Esther visited each other through their student years. This led to a deepening of their friendship and the formation of other friendships between other family members. Monica and her husband came to Esther and Dev's wedding with Monica's Dad and Step Mum; who are now our close friends. When Monica got married in Switzerland, we were invited too. We are so blessed to have friends from such diverse backgrounds that bring a richness into our lives.

30

Dad Finished His Race

Following mum's death, Dad was really ill for a while and unable to manage on his own. This is always a difficult time for families and we were no different. We wanted to help him stay in his own home; to be able to go to the church he knew but it became obvious it was not safe. He would wake up at night and think it was day. He would be on the phone in the early hours, saying he was unable to get his TV on or make himself something to eat. He would forget he had put a pan on the hob and burn the bottom out. So, there was an increasing risk of fire. Dad was becoming more insecure and scared. He needed people around him.

I was still working at Princess Royal hospital and often on call and working nights. It seemed right to try and find Dad a place somewhere nearby, so Barrie and I could visit easily and often. The family agreed. We suggested to dad that he tried a couple of weeks respite at a lovely residential home near us. He loved it. Both the staff and the residents made such a fuss of him and it was not long before he wanted to stay. We were all able to visit him and take him out for trips to the shops or for lunch. I could call in on my way home from work and often found him engaged in conversation with other residents. He was happy. We were relieved.

Dad stayed in this lovely home until he died just before Christmas 2009.

I must tell you about God's amazing timing. I had decided that I would retire from my job at the hospital at the end of 2009. I was only 63 but it had been muted at work that we should move to doing 12-hour shifts. The job was demanding and required much concentration to avoid making mistakes. The thought of having to keep that level of concentration up for a 12-hour day gave me cause for concern. I handed in my notice with this in mind. I was obliged to give three months' notice, but in fact I gave them four as it is not always easy to find a replacement.

The staff asked me what sort of leaving do would I like? To which I replied that I did not want any fuss – I came quietly and I wanted to go quietly. But not a chance. The morning of my last day I walked into the staff room to find it decked high and low with balloons, streamers and messages. They had prepared a buffet lunch with speeches and thanks. People who were not demonstrative actually gave me hugs and kisses. A large gift of money with other presents were presented along with an invitation to a retirement meal at a local Hotel, just after the Christmas holidays. Well, if that is going quietly, I wondered what the alternative would look like?

It's strange that you can work with people for years and not know how they feel about you until you leave. This was quite moving. When I drove home after my last shift, I was mulling this over, but I can also remember thinking, no more night duties, no more on calls. The latter were pleasant and comforting thoughts.

I had some time owing that I had not been able to take advantage of, so I took those days before my retirement date. Barrie and I had planned a long holiday when I retired, to visit relatives in Australia, New Zealand and India. We were going to be away for a couple of months from the end of January to the end of March. There was however a large shadow over head. I was concerned about Dad. I had not told him at that point we were going because I did not want him to get upset. I was also worried about anything happening to him and not being there to help, perhaps even having to come home part way through the holiday. So many worries were going through my mind. I felt guilty about going away and leaving him.

God knew all about these concerns. Dad's life was drawing to a close. He rapidly went downhill with an infection that did not respond to treatment. He had reached the grand old age of 92 and had been able to enjoy life to the full until a few days before he died in his own bed, at the home that he had come to know and love. Taking the few days leave that I was owed, meant that for dads last days on earth, I was able to spend the time with him. I was there until the moment God took him home and was so grateful to have been there to see him on his journey.

It almost seems surreal when I think about it. Dad's room was on the first floor and I needed to let the night staff know that dad had died. I was making my way down the corridor and met an old lady wandering around. She said to me:

I don't know where my room is. Can you help me find it?

I tried to explain that I was not a staff member but she shouted:

You don't care about me; I am nothing to you.

I offered to find a staff member to help her and scurried down the stairs thinking:

My dad has just died; this is all very strange!

I found a night attendant and explained both situations and left it all in his care. I was suddenly so tired and needed to get home for a shoulder to cry on. Even in the early hours Barrie was there for me.

As soon as we were able, we contacted my sister and brother; along with other people, to let them know that Dad had gone to be with his Saviour. We were able to clear Dad's room with help from the staff at the home and we registered his death. My sister and I arranged the funeral and the service at Dad's old church in Shrewsbury. Our brother George lives in High Wickham so was happy to leave the arrangements to us. The timing was so amazing but you might be wondering, why the rush? Everything needed to be done before the necessary offices closed down for the Christmas holidays. The timing was important because of attending Dad's funeral, before our flight to Australia

Barrie and I were able to go on holiday without any worries about Dad, as he was in the Lord's care. I never did tell him that we were going away; he made his journey before ours began.

31

The Retirement Trip

We had planned the first leg of our trip to begin in Australia. I wanted to visit my cousin Joan who lives not far from Sidney, in the Blue Mountains. I had not seen her for so many years; I wondered if we would recognise each other. No problem there, it was as if we had seen each other last week. It was quite moving to talk with her about my dad (her uncle) and his last few days on earth. Joan's husband had died a few years earlier and we shared together the hope Christians have, that one day we will all meet up again. The time flew by but we were able to have a short look around before flying to New Zealand, the second leg of our journey.

We were met at the airport by our niece and family and taken on a short sightseeing drive before going back to their home. My sister and brother-in-law have three children, girl, boy, girl. The two youngest live with their families not far apart from each other on New Zealand's South Island. Prior to our trip they had asked us what we would like to do and see whilst with them. We had expressed the wish to see New Zealand as the local people see it. They organised tours of both the North and the South Islands, with accommodation ranging from a 'bed in a shed' to five-star hotels and everything in between. They organised routes, ferries and car hire. They arranged every detail missing nothing that was required. It was a masterpiece of planning and we still had plenty of time to spend with them, catch up on all the news and play with the children. But all too soon it was over. The goodbyes were really difficult and emotional. None of us knew when we would see each other again. There were lots of hugs and tears as we finally boarded our plane and then we were on the third leg of the trip, to Singapore. On the plane I reflected on the mixed emotions; the joy and excitement in arrivals and the pain and sadness in departures. I also thought that I would not want to miss either, as they are an important part of living life to the full.

Many people love Singapore but I was too distracted to really enjoy it. My thoughts and feelings were back in New Zealand. We visited the Orchid house, did some shopping and took loads of photos which we have had time to mull over since. I am pleased to have seen and experienced it but have no desire to visit again. There are other places I would like to see.

We boarded a flight to Delhi on the fourth leg of the journey. The plan was that we would meet Esther, Dev, Amrit and Maninder (Dev's mum and dad) at the airport. This was our first time in India but more importantly, Esther had not met many of her new family since she and Dev had married. They were flying in to Delhi and were due to arrive about an hour before we landed. The timing was a bit tight and when we walked through the barriers, we could not see any one of them. We walked through the crowded hall, past a rather tall Indian man and noticed he was holding up a large placard with Buzz Light Year i.e., Professor Freud and Princess Royal written on it. Rather strange we thought until it dawned on us that those were the nick names Maninder had given us. As we stopped, they all jumped out from behind him. This rather big man was Maninder's nephew. It's not just us who like to play a trick or two; they all enjoyed the look of surprise on our faces. I also noticed the questions written across the faces of people in the crowd; Who are these people, Princess Royal and Professor Freud?

I think the word 'surprise' really sums up our visit to India. The mini bus they had hired to carry us and our luggage, for the duration of our visit was something else. It was complete with red velvet curtains with gold tassels, pictures of various Gurus hanging in the windscreen and other places and a bed in the back. What more could one want? It all seemed larger than life and with loud Bhangra music playing and every one tooting their horns, we drove the 5-hour journey from Delhi to the Punjab. We passed six people on a moped; a man, a woman sitting side saddle with a baby on her knee, a child on the handle bars, one on the cross bar and another behind the lady. We saw a man balancing a table top whilst riding his motor bike. People were living in huts by the road side, washing and bathing in small tubs. People were working in the fields; the ladies worked wearing brightly coloured saris or silvar suits. This was a different and fascinating world!

We arrived at the nephew's home to a royal welcome. He lives with his family in the village of Mahalpur. They had kindly given up their own room for us to use but we did not know that they slept on boards. Our night was very interesting for a couple who were used to the home comfort of a mattress. When Amrit realised the situation, a mattress appeared the following night.

After enjoying the experience of life in this Indian village and meeting several relatives we travelled on to the village of Phoriwaluld. There we stayed with Maninder's mother's relatives. Their village is close to the busy city of Jalandahar, an amazing place to shop. The experience of sitting down or even lying down, being served drinks and food whilst buying material for saris, jewellery or anything else, was different to say the least. But it was really enjoyable. Then came the bartering over the cost until a mutual agreement was reached. I had never seen this process conducted in quite this way before. The women were as good at bartering as the men. With wagging fingers, shaking heads and loud retorts of NEH NEY NEYs the business was eventually completed.

This family lived in a very old farm, with the buildings forming a rectangle around a central area, open to the sun. Cooking, washing, socialising, and play etc all happened in the central, communal area for most of the year. Everyone was eager to meet us and get us to try the local delicacies. We had babies placed on our knees and photos taken with so many strangers. In these areas, they didn't have many white visitors. Even when we dressed in their local costumes, it was hard to go unnoticed.

Having been asked if there was anything that I would like to do whilst in India? I replied that I would like to milk a cow. Well, everyone has a bucket list no matter how strange. Ok they said and arranged for me to visit the 'Koo'(Indian for farm). They considered my clothes to be too good for this job, so they found me a pale pink silvar suite complete with sparkly beads! I thought that this was far better than my clothes, but not to argue, I put it on. Now they do not sit whilst milking, they squat. I found this position quite hard because it pulls the leg muscles and it is easier to lose balance (Before you ask, NO I did not fall over in the poop). They had tied the back legs of a cow together and also those of a buffalo. It stops them kicking out. I had a go milking both but obviously not at the same time. It was such fun and eventually I got the hang of it. I felt a bit sorry for the animals but I am sure they both recovered. Everyone was really amused and said that when I returned to India, that would be my job.

I don't think so. It would take me all day: I thought.

After a few more days of rest, Maninder said that we were going on tour to see the sights. It was wonderful to have people with us who knew the languages, places and culture. So, it was back in the Charabanc and on the way to Delhi. Amongst some of the places we visited were the huge Red Fort, the Taj Palace and Safdarjang's Tomb. People did not seem to worry about dropping litter. Everywhere we went, the streets were strewn with rubbish. However, the beauty of the architecture, the skill of the Indian craftsmen and women was evident to be seen and wondered at. The energy of the city with the noise of its erratic traffic, its many tuck tucks, residents and tourists, was strangely endearing.

Leaving Delhi, we moved on and travelled to Rajasthan. This provided a great contrast to other areas as it was brown, dry and mountainous. The men wore a different style turban which was not entirely enclosed but had an open area in the centre. The area of Jaipur is well known for its amazing jewellery, silver, gold and jewels; its marquetry with wood and mother of Pearl and its fabulous mosaics. Also well known in this area is the Amber palace. It is situated high up on a mountain side with elephants ferrying people up the steep and winding path to its entrance. This was like going back in time with something like the 'Great Wall of China' marking out the miles of palace boundaries.

Now to contrast the old with the new. We booked to stay at a luxury hotel with every modern convenience mixed with Indian architecture and charm. As our Charabanc drove along the impressive drive to this magnificent building, we noticed a reception committee standing outside waiting. Who are they waiting for I wondered? It was us. We were greeted by an Indian piper playing an Indian melody, the manager standing on a red carpet and waiters with glasses of Champagne.

During our stay the manager asked Barrie how he liked the hotel?

Barrie replied: It is just like being at home.

I really don't know what picture that conjured up for him of where and how we lived, but we certainly had the VIP treatment during our stay.

Everyone talks about the beauty of the Taj Mahal at Agra. So, we went to see it for ourselves. Yes, it is really beautiful. Was it the highlight of our trip? Not really because we had already seen many other places in India that we felt were equally as wonderful. But it was worth seeing.

Having been to many ancient places, we went to see a new city. A visit to the city of Chandigarh. Here it is a crime to drop litter, so the streets were clean. It was whilst here we visited another relative, a retired Colonel from the Indian army. He and his wife lived in a beautiful modern house and invited us to share a meal with them. Their son and daughter had also come to meet us and it was so lovely to see how they cared for each other. The Colonel's wife was really ill. She seemed to be unable to talk but nodded and smiled. They graciously allowed us to pray for her before we left.

Our visit to the Punjab would not have been complete without visit to the Golden Temple at Amritsar. It is the most important religious site to the Sikhs. On route we drove through a rocky area that is inhabited by hundreds of very playful monkeys. I think they found us as interesting as we did them. They jumped all over the passing cars – those that slowed down long enough to look at them. The Temple is surrounded by a lake and many believe the water cleanses away their sicknesses. It was really impressive – covered with gold leaf and gleaming in the sun. People were queuing just to be able to enter it.

We are so pleased to have had the privilege and pleasure of visiting these amazing places. To see the animals, inspiring gardens with their exotic plants was wonderful, but, the most wonderful of all, was meeting these warm hearted and very beautiful people.

It was a holiday to be remembered, but we were ready to be reunited with other family members and friends. It had been the longest holiday we had ever had and probably, would ever have. Relatives that live close to Heathrow airport had taken care of our cars. Once we had collected them, we were on our way home. The roads and traffic seemed very orderly and quiet. The difference between India and England was so noticeable. Every one kept to their side of the road and there were no horns blowing.

32

A Not so Hidden Talent

Helen has always loved reading and although she hated school, she never lost her passion for books and her ability to be very creative. As their boys were growing up, she decided that she would begin to study again. After doing a foundation course she began to study for a degree with Open University in English Language and Literature. She gained her degree with honours in 2013. By then she was well and truly into studying. She continued and got her teaching qualifications also. To add to her many gifts, she has developed the ability to recognise when students are struggling and know how to motivate them to achieve their goals.

After starting work at Shrewsbury Technical College, she literally began to fly. She has now attained her Masters and teaches on degree and post graduate education programmes. When birds take to the sky there is no telling where the wind will carry them. We use an expression, 'The Sky is the limit'. I think that this is appropriate in Helen's case and only God knows what's next. Helen's story is a real encouragement to those who did not get on well at school.

33

A Chance Meeting?

An Introduction to House of Prayer

Whilst at a Grandparents day organised by the school of some of our grandchildren, we met an older couple who were part of a church in Wellington. Their Pastors had moved from a church in Shrewsbury and planted a new church in Wellington. We had met these church planters for the first time whilst at the Good News Crusade camps and again in Shrewsbury. They were really very special people. We had also known the older couple for a considerable number of years. Here they were, sitting just in front of us on these very low children's chairs. Not bad I thought for oldies, that is until it came time to get up. The second action was obviously more difficult than the first for quite a few of us.

Their Pastors had just retired in 2012 and passed the leadership of the church to Tony and Mary. Our paths had crossed with Tony and Mary over the years, so we were interested to find out how they were doing. The older couple suggested that we visit 'House of Prayer' and see for ourselves. Good idea, we thought.

We decided to go a couple of weeks later and got caught up into the heavenlies during the worship. The time flew by and we could not wait to visit again. The welcome was warm and it was like a home coming. During the next few years, we were invited to take part in preaching, teaching and pastoral work. However, we felt that all we wanted to do was rest in the Lord's presence, which was so evident there. The older couple that we had met at the grandparents' day were helping on the 'Greeters' rota i.e., welcoming people to the Sunday services. They were going to be away on holiday and needed someone to do their welcoming slot. We were asked if we would help, just as a one off you understand? Well, we had heard that somewhere before. That was the start.

Other members of the group that met in our home had become curious as to where we were going and gradually joined us on a Sunday at the House of Prayer. We continue to meet as a home group during the week, that is covid 19 permitting.

One weekend a guest speaker was due to do a Saturday afternoon session. This was the first time I had felt that we should attend something other than the Sunday Service. It was so right we were there, as this lovely man had a prophetic word for Barrie. How encouraging that was. It resulted in a change taking place in us. We now felt like we could get more involved. It was not long before we were invited to join the leadership of this lovely church family. We finally accepted and have served as part of this leadership team to the present day.

So, was this just another chance meeting with this older couple or more of another God incidence?

34

Friendships Bonded

The couple, Jonathan and Pam, who visited House of Prayer and spoke that Saturday afternoon have become friends. It happens sometimes, that you just hit it off with people. A surprise blessing that God had up His sleeve.

We wanted Pam and Jonathan to meet some friends who have a farm near the Mid Wales coast. The farm mostly rears sheep and is situated in a beautiful, rather wild unspoilt valley. The valley had experienced revival and revival meetings had actually been held on the farm. Later a small Methodist chapel was built a few hundred yards down the road. It was needed to accommodate the increasing number of people who came to know Jesus. Unfortunately, over the years the number of worshipers dwindled and the chapel was no longer needed. It has since been made into lovely holiday accommodation.

I had booked a small Welsh cottage, for the four us to stay for three nights. It was not too far from the farm. We were all in holiday mood with the food for our self-catering break tightly packed in the boot, along with our luggage.

On arrival it seemed really small but very quaint. It had one bedroom with a bed settee downstairs. An open fire with the logs to burn, a compact kitchen and a small bathroom all added to the cosy atmosphere. With hills to the front and back, the setting was wonderful.

Jonathan came down to the bathroom the first morning and a notice on the bathroom door caught his eye. It seemed to be the calendar for the cottage bookings. He asked:

Do you know who Lynn so and so is?

We had never heard of this lady but Jonathan went on to say,

Well, she is arriving on Wednesday.

What! We exclaimed.

It was Tuesday already and we were not planning to leave until Thursday. Where were our names; what had happened to our booking? Jonathan found our booking for the same dates but unfortunately for the following month. Oh no, how had that happened? This posed the question of where would we stay on Wednesday night? Worse still, if being here and not expected, we could be classified as squatters!

I felt so stupid, how could this have happened? But we needed somewhere to stay and my thoughts went to the lovely little chapel near the farm. I wondered if it was available. We asked our friends on the farm for the owner's telephone number but we could not get hold of her through the day. Time was running out.

That evening Jonathan was due to speak to a prayer group that met in a hall adjoining the Chapel in

Aberdovey. This was a mostly Welsh speaking group so it was going to be interesting as none of us could speak Welsh. However, our friends from the farm would be there and their son was leading the meeting. Once there and seated around this huge table, it felt like we were really small with everyone placed so far apart.

Understandably the conversation was not easy, so the silences felt protracted and uncomfortable. Jonathan whispered to us that he felt out of his depth to which we replied:

Don't worry we are here.

I really don't know what difference we thought that would make, but it seemed like the right thing to say at the time. The group sang hymns in Welsh and English and then Jonathan was introduced. It was wonderful. Jonathan spoke about their history of revival and won their hearts. He was sharing about things they knew and things they treasured. He led them to think about what God wanted next, in the present, and for the future. You could visibly see people warming and after the meeting we were offered a look round the lovely chapel next door. It was great to chat to the people over a cup of tea and know that God had brought us together for this short time for His purposes. We arrived as strangers but left as friends.

We still did not have anywhere to stay the following night so I needed to try and ring again. It was dark as we left the prayer meeting. Under the glow of a street light, I put my hand bag on the ground to rummage for my phone and the number. Kneeling on the pavement and talking to Pam, Jonathan and Barrie, I turned to see why they hadn't replied. They had walked on and I had been talking to myself whilst kneeling at the road side. They were nowhere to be seen. What would you think if you had witnessed a woman on her knees at the side of the road, in the dark talking to herself? Well, the good news was I managed to get through and fixed up the accommodation for the following night! Relief.

We left the cottage immaculate the following day. No one would have known we had ever been there. We never did meet Lynn but she had a shiny clean place in which to stay and the squatters were long gone.

Out on the hills of this lovely valley we prayed together that revival would again visit this beautiful place. We asked God to release the Angels, that had once been so busy in the area, to help with those who were being saved.

That evening we spent some time at the chapel (holiday accommodation) with our friends from the farm. On his way home, the son (a very grounded young man) stopped his quad bike to open the farm gate and happened to look up. Just above him was a huge Angel with a trumpet. The sight took his breath away. How can anyone account for this. He did not know we had been out in the valley praying about angels. The next day we spent some time at the farm praying for them and the valley, before making our way back to Newport.

35

Special celebration

In 2018, we celebrated our 50 Golden Wedding anniversary. When we were newly married, we often used to say to each other with a smile:

Will you still love me when I am old and grey?

Well, we don't say that anymore because we are old and grey. When we look back, we wonder where all those years have gone? Then we begin to remember some of the adventures we have had together and give God thanks.

People came from up and down the country and from abroad to celebrate with us. We had a marque in Kate and Luke's garden and a bouncy Castle; which I am tempted to say was for the children, but that's not strictly speaking true. I had a great time on it, as did quite a few of the adults. My brother came dressed as a page boy, not quite the same as on our wedding day but close. The weather was wonderful, the food amazing but the greatest treasure of all was the fellowship of family and friends.

Grandchildren

Esther and Dev now have three amazing children, two girls and a boy. The two eldest celebrated our Golden anniversary with us. The youngest was born a year or so later. So, we now have twelve wonderful grandchildren; three granddaughters and nine grandsons. The twelfth grandson is adopted. Erica and Craig's nephew was upset not having a grandad. His last biological grandad had died and the other young people he mixes with at school, all had a grandad. This was really affecting him so he asked if Jo and Iona's grandad would also be his? Now we have the twelfth grandchild. What a joy to watch them grow and develop. Our eldest grandson is driving and has taken us out for a spin. Two more are learning to drive so I expect we will get another outing or two in the not-too-distant future.

36

Prophecy Plays Its Part

There have been many times through our lives when God has spoken through a prophetic word. Let me tell you about just a few of those times.

Whilst at a Christian gathering the speaker, writer, and prophet, Jim/James Goll (cofounder of Encounters Network) prophesied over me. Amongst the things he said was that I was an (like) Anna and would pray in the end time prophecies. As you probably know Anna was a prophetess in the temple in Jerusalem with Simeon[12]. They had both been waiting and praying for the promised Messiah. When Joseph and Mary brought Jesus to the temple, they recognised the baby Jesus as the long awaited, the promised Messiah. This was Jesus' first coming but the end time prophecies tell of His second coming[13].

At the time Jim Goll brought that word for me, some people did not recognise me as an Anna (i.e., having prophetic gifting) and wanted to change the name in Jim's prophecy from Anna to Hannah[14] (a lady in the Bible who prayed for a child). I did not want to be pigeon holed as either, so I filed the prophecy out of sight until more recent times.

It is interesting how God often speaks to people about a future time. The words become true even if they are not evident in the present. Some people in the Bible were called mighty warriors long before they engaged in battle.

On another Occasion – we were at a retreat; a wonderful place named the 'House of Bread' in the Cotswolds. The manager of the centre is a lovely young man. He with others, form a small Christian Community and as such, they pray for each group prior to their arrival. He did an introduction on the first evening explaining the safety procedures and other things our group needed to know.

On this occasion in 2018, the manager shared a wonderful testimony about a friend of his. This friend lives in Canada and he became very ill and died on the operating table. He was certified as dead after 20 minutes. The medical staff had tried to resuscitate with no success and he was being prepared to be taken down to the morgue.

During these 20 minutes, the friend had visited heaven and Jesus had told him that he could not stay but was being sent back with an important message to deliver to the Midlands UK. The message was that God was going to visit the Midlands again with the power, healings and miracles that many had witnessed in the sixties and seventies. This was a new season. The manager's friend had visited him recently at the House of Bread, and then went on from there to deliver the message as God had directed. As we were from the Midlands, the manager shared it with us. If God felt that the message was so important that He raised someone from the dead, then we needed to take notice.

For two nights prior to this retreat the Lord had been speaking to me about a 'New Season'. So, you can imagine that my ears picked up when the prophecy was shared. Another God incidence?

A Word for Barrie. I have mentioned that Jonathan gave Barrie a prophetic word at a meeting one Saturday afternoon but I did not mention what it was. Well, Jonathan had seen Barrie as a painting that was being restored to its original beauty. Over the years the painting had suffered damage, some as a result of time and some from the attempts of others to alter it; to paint over it. God was putting it back to His original design. The prophetic word resonated with Barrie in such a way, that it gave him permission to be himself. The new freedom enabled him to engage once again in what God had planned for him.

Recently, during this 2021 lock down, there has been a growing awareness amongst people, of our need for one another. People in nursing and residential homes have not been able to see their loved ones. People in or visiting hospital, have been separated from the support of family who care for them. There are those who are shielding, who feel isolated and those who would just love a hug. They are all saying the same thing, that they miss each other. In what was our very independent, self-sufficient country there is a change taking place. There is an increasing recognition of the blight of loneliness and our need of family and friends.

A friend, who is prophetic shared with us that he felt God is pressing the reset button. With a computer or other electrical devises, I understand that the reset set button causes the equipment to default back to the maker's original settings. Over the years we tweak things, add things and change things. Sometimes it works but the way something is designed to function is usually the best.

Over time, we have grown to appreciate the makers hand book for all creation. His design for our living is to be found in the Bible.

Do I understand it all?

No, I don't, but I do know that God loves me and wants the best for me. Just like any loving parent would want the best for their children.

Do I know what the future holds?

Well, not everything, but I know who holds the future. I know He is faithful and that as we walk together here on earth, we will continue our journey with Him in heaven. Jesus said that he was going to prepare a place for us, and that there are many rooms in His Father's house. I believe it. He wants us to be with Him. This is the City that Abraham was looking for, whose builder and architect is God[2].

At the time of writing this I am 74 years old and Barrie 79. Our story runs across all those years. Yet I have written in just a few pages what has taken years to live out. You can read in just an hour or two, a journey that covers a life time. Because of the number of miracles, we have witnessed, it would be easy to give the impression that we have lived somewhere above reality; so much so that we must be out of touch with ordinary people. I hope that's not the case, as life still has to be lived. The cleaning, washing, cooking and general chores still need doing and those things level the playing field for all of us. We share in our mutual humanity but at the same time we can touch heaven.

Barrie intends to retire from Church leadership on his eightieth birthday and I will retire a year or so later. Or at least that is the plan. We are transitioning from parent to grandparent mode. We have lived a wonderful, full and active life. To experience what Jesus calls life abundant does not mean fantasy or pretence but to live and experience everything from birth to death, sadness and joy, plenty and little, ease and struggle. To share life with Jesus and enjoy the journey as it unfolds is our joy and passion. My prayer for you, reader, is that you will experience life together with Him and the joy that brings.

References

1. Abraham Genesis 11;27

2. Hebrews 11;10 to 12;5 The city whose architect and builder was God

3. Acts 8;27 – 40

4. Prayer to receive Salvation

   Jesus, I believe You are the Son of God. Thank You for dying on the cross and taking my sin upon yourself. I willingly and unreservedly forgive those who have hurt me. Please forgive me for all the wrong things I have done, thought and spoken. I turn away from those things now and renounce any involvement in the occult also false religions and their gods. Please cleans me and come to live in me and be my Saviour. I thank You Jesus.

5. Speaking in Tongues Acts 2;4

6. Words of Knowledge and gifts of Holy Spirit. 1 Cor 12;8-10.

7. Nicodemus. The Gospel of John 3;1-13

8. Angels rejoice over one sinner that repents. Luke 15;10

9. Speaking the truth in love. Ephesians 4;15

10. Angels help the heirs of Salvation. Hebrews 1;14

11. Ezekiel 37;9. Come from the Four Winds.

12. Luke 2;21-39

13. Acts 1;11

14. 1 Sam 1 . . .